Science and Technology: How Things Work

by Deborah Crotts

illustrated by Joseph Dolce

FS-10169 Science and Technology: How Things Work
All rights reserved–Printed in the U.S.A.
Copyright © 1995 Frank Schaffer Publications, Inc.
23740 Hawthorne Blvd.
Torrance, CA 90505

Table of Contents

Introduction

Science and Technology: How Things Work is intended to be an enrichment resource to serve as a companion to the classroom text. It contains activities and experiments designed to teach scientific principles as well as the *how* and *why* of applied science over a wide range of topics. Some of the activities demonstrate the principles behind current technology; others are models or demonstrations of actual inventions. The exercises stress the application of science, using hands-on activities which stimulate creative thought and stretch students' thinking beyond the confines of the classroom. The activities deal with machines and topics students encounter in everyday living as well as topics outside the average range of experience.

These activities demonstrate that science is an active, ongoing process in which everyone can participate, not a static compendium of knowledge to be absorbed by rote learning or restricted to a chosen few. Students will see the usefulness of science in every facet of their lives and discover first-hand the underlying principles that govern the technology we possess.

The activities can be used individually to support the various topics in the classroom text or can be developed as a separate supplementary unit of study. In the Teacher Notes, suggestions are given for follow-up activities, bulletin board ideas, and research topics to coordinate with the individual activities and with the chapters as a whole unit.

Each activity was chosen to capitalize on high student interest. The activities require only inexpensive, easily obtainable materials and need only minimal teacher supervision. All activities are easy and safe to perform. Any cautionary information is highlighted.

Each student activity sheet is a self-contained, reproducible unit. Materials for each experiment or activity are listed at the top of each student page and any substitutions or alternate suggestions are offered in the Teacher Notes which are at the front of each chapter. Patterns are included where applicable. The Teacher Notes also contain supplementary background information to introduce or expand the topic being presented. The answer keys for all student activity sheets are found in the back of the book.

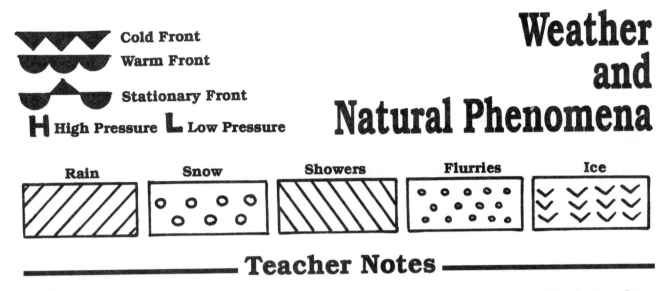

Chapter One

Weather and Natural Phenomena

- Cold Front
- Warm Front
- Stationary Front
- **H** High Pressure **L** Low Pressure

Rain | Snow | Showers | Flurries | Ice

Teacher Notes

The activities in this chapter are concerned with the instruments and effects of weather and natural phenomena. Use this chapter to set up your own classroom weather station. Mount a world map and a map of your state on a bulletin board and have the students use construction paper to make larger versions of the weather symbols at the top of this page. Bring in weather forecasts from the local newspaper and appoint students to listen to the daily weather report on television and radio and present this information to the class. Use push pins to fasten the symbols in the appropriate places on the maps to correspond with these weather reports. Note and discuss discrepancies and keep a record of the accuracy of the different reports.

An indoor/outdoor thermometer and a barometer should be purchased for a basic weather station. Students can make a rain gauge from a narrow jar or can or you can purchase one. Students can use the anemometer and the windsock from the activity sheets in this chapter to determine approximate wind velocity and direction. Use the following chart to determine cloud types:

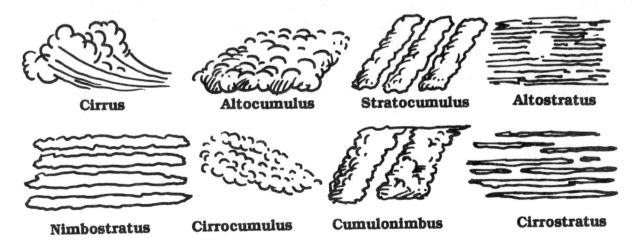

Cirrus | Altocumulus | Stratocumulus | Altostratus

Nimbostratus | Cirrocumulus | Cumulonimbus | Cirrostratus

Have students predict the weather independent of newspaper, radio, and television forecasts. Record their predictions and compare their success rate with that of the professional weather forecasters. Keep a daily record of the actual weather and note trends. Consult an almanac for normal and record temperature and precipitation in your area, as well as average annual snow and rainfall and average and fastest wind speeds for your area.

Additionally, have students research the formation of sleet, hail, and snowflakes. What is the difference? Collect snowflakes on a piece of cold glass and study them with a magnifying glass. Have students make drawings of different snowflake shapes.

Also discuss safety measures for any dangerous weather which is common to your area. Make certain that students understand the difference between the terms *weather watch* and *weather warning*.

The Weather

This activity sheet encourages student research. What are the typical weather patterns of your area? What freak storms and weather patterns have occurred in your area? Cyclones, hurricanes, tornadoes, floods, and blizzards are common in our country. The mountain ranges with the plains area in between provide a perfect stage for weather extremes. When winds reach a mountain range, they blow up one side and blow down the other. The wind blowing up the range pulls rain with it, giving an extra amount of rainfall to that side of the mountain range. The down side of the range gets less precipitation than average, leading to drought or desert conditions. A cyclone occurs when a cold and a warm front are moving away from each other. A partial vacuum or low pressure area forms in the middle and starts to pull the two fronts back toward each other. The cold air starts pouring in one side of the low pressure and the warm air pours in the other side and the whole system rotates. Have students research some of these more outstanding cyclones in recent history: January, 1969, when 10 days of rain brought floods and mudslides in California; November, 1982–April, 1983, when a series of cyclones brought high winds, large waves, rain, and tornadoes to southern and central California and blizzards to Colorado; and February, 1986, when 12 days of rain flooded California.

Thunderstorms top the list of dangerous weather phenomena. On August 15, 1967, lightning started the Sundance fire in the Selkirk Mountains of Idaho, destroying 56,000 acres. On August 23 and 24, 1970, thunderstorms started 100 separate fires in the Cascade Mountains in Washington. These fires burned 100,000 acres of land. On July 6, 1985, a lightning bolt struck a generating plant in Salt Lake City and left much of Utah without electricity. On July 27, 1985, lightning struck a group of hikers who were climbing Half Dome in Yosemite National Park, California. Two hikers were killed. Another hiker in Sequoia National Park was killed by lightning that same day.

Thermometer

This activity demonstrates the principles behind the thermometer. If the cap to the bottle is too thick or stiff to puncture easily, a piece of plastic wrap four layers thick or a heavier piece of plastic from a trash bag may be stretched tightly over the opening and secured with a rubber band. Puncture the plastic wrap or plastic carefully with the point of very sharp scissors and insert the straw in the opening. Seal the straw in the opening with the Silly Putty, being careful to keep the wrap or plastic taut across the mouth of the bottle.

Follow this activity by discussing how heat makes solids, liquids, and gases expand and cold makes them contract. If the weather outside is cold, purchase a helium balloon and take it outdoors. What happens to the balloon? (It deflates.) What happens to a slightly flat helium balloon in a hot car on a sunny day? (It inflates.)

Hygrometer

Since human hair expands and contracts with the humidity, a long hair makes an ideal hygrometer. This model demonstrates the change in the humidity with the movement of the toothpick indicator needle.

The hair does not need to be extremely long. If the donor has exceptionally long hair, consider cutting the hair in two pieces to make two hygrometers from one donation.

Barometer

This model barometer will not measure normal changes in barometric pressure. Have a working barometer on hand to show to students to introduce this activity. After completion of the student activity sheet, have students make a 21-day chart. Use the working barometer to keep a three-week record of the barometric pressure and compare it to the weather. Have students check the barometer every 15 to 30 minutes on a day when a rain shower is expected. (If you have a window with a good view of the sky and see a storm approaching, appoint a student to monitor the barometric changes.)

Windsock

After completion of this activity sheet, discuss the difference between a windsock and a weather vane. Are there other ways to determine the direction and velocity of the wind? (A moist finger held up in the air can help you determine wind direction and an anemometer and visual cues can help you determine wind velocity.) Have students record the direction of the wind when a storm is approaching. From which direction do most of your storms come?

Anemometer

This activity allows students to make a working model anemometer. The scale at the bottom of the student page varies in accuracy depending on the elasticity of the rubber band. Use ¼-inch-thick rubber bands. (Check with your post office if you cannot find them in your office supply store. The bands used by the mail carriers to hold small bundles of letters and magazines work very well.)

Severe storms are associated with high winds (and dramatic changes in barometric pressure). Have students research tornadoes, derechos (severe windstorms with winds of 58 miles per hour or stronger which damage an area at least 280 miles long), hurricanes, and thunderstorms. Which storms are most common to your area? What are the dangers from each different storm? What signs indicate the approach of one of these storms? How can you protect yourself from one of these storms?

Seismograph

To introduce this activity, discuss recent earthquakes and the concept of tectonic plates. What fault lines are located near you? Explain that an earthquake causes rippling movements in the earth similar to ripples caused by a pebble dropped into a pool of still water. (Demonstrate this by dropping a pebble into a wide shallow pan of water. Let students observe the ripples.) The ripples form a wavy-shaped line, with the farthest ripple being shortest in height. The seismograph measures the height or amplitude of this ripple.

Measuring Earthquakes

Discuss the different scales and the reasons for using each scale to measure earthquakes. Be certain that students understand the difference between magnitude (the amount of energy given off by the earthquake) and intensity (the effects or damage produced by the quake). Discuss the need for special engineering for structures built near fault lines and the need for special building codes in these areas. For additional research, have students investigate the tsunami or seismic sea wave and some of these famous earthquakes in the United States: 1886 in Charleston, South Carolina; 1906 in California; 1964 in southern Alaska; 1989 in California.

The Weather

Rain	Snow	Showers	Flurries	Ice

1. Why is it important to study about weather?

   _____

   _____

2. How quickly can weather patterns change?

   _____

   _____

3. Do the weather reporters and national weather forecasters always know what weather is coming for a given area?

   _____

   _____

4. What is the worst you can expect for your area in terms of weather? Use a current almanac or other library resources to find out when the last thunderstorms, tornadoes, hurricanes, blizzards, cyclones, floods, tidal waves, or droughts affected your area. What sort of bad weather is most likely for your area? What is least likely?

   _____

   _____

   _____

5. What instruments do weather forecasters use to determine the weather? See if you can name the most necessary instruments and what they are used for.

   a. _____

   b. _____

   c. _____

   d. _____

   e. _____

Thermometer

Materials: A small, clear glass bottle, a narrow, clear plastic straw, Silly Putty, ice cubes, hot tap water, cold tap water, two bowls, rubbing alcohol, a marker, and food coloring.

Procedure:

1. Fill the glass bottle half full of alcohol. Add two or three drops of food coloring and swish the bottle **gently** to mix it.

Silly Putty

2. Punch a hole in the top to the bottle and insert the straw through the hole. Make a ring of Silly Putty around the straw to seal the opening. (See diagram at right.)

3. Use the marker to mark the height of the alcohol in the straw.

4. Hold the bottle in your hand for several minutes. As the liquid in the bottle warms, what happens? Mark the level of the alcohol in the straw.

   _____

5. Place the cold water and ice cubes in one bowl. Set the bottle in the center of the ice water for a few minutes. What happens? Mark the level of the alcohol in the straw.

   _____

6. Place the hot tap water in the other bowl. Set the bottle in the center of the hot water for a few minutes. What happens? Mark the level of the alcohol in the straw.

   _____

Evaluate:

1. What makes the alcohol move higher in the straw? _____

   _____

   _____

2. How does a mercury or alcohol thermometer work? _____

   _____

   _____

Hygrometer

A hygrometer measures the humidity or the amount of moisture in the air. A simple hygrometer is easy to make. This hygrometer will not tell you the amount of humidity in the air but it will tell you when there is more or less humidity.

Materials: A clean, clear glass jar, a Popsicle stick, a toothpick, tape, a marker, and one long human hair.

Procedure:

1. With the marker, color one end of the toothpick.

2. Wrap one end of the hair around the center of the toothpick. Fasten it to the toothpick with a piece of tape.

3. Wrap the other end of the hair around the center of the Popsicle stick. Make certain the distance between the Popsicle stick and the toothpick is less than the height of the jar. The toothpick needs to be suspended in the jar and be free to swing around. Secure the hair to the Popsicle stick with tape.

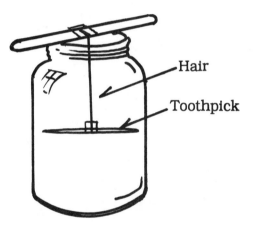

4. Hang the Popsicle stick over the jar opening so the toothpick is suspended in the middle of the jar as in the illustration to the right.

5. Place the jar where it will not be moved or jostled. When the toothpick has stopped moving, carefully mark the point on the jar where the colored tip of the toothpick is pointing. What is the weather like?

_____

_____

6. Check on your hygrometer daily, recording any changes in the direction of the toothpick. Your toothpick hygrometer will point one way on humid days and another on dry days. Why do you think this happens?

_____

_____

Barometer

Materials: A small glass jar, a toothpick, glue, plastic wrap, a rubber band, and a straw.

Procedure:

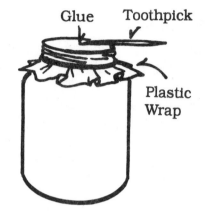

Glue   Toothpick

Plastic Wrap

1. Cover the jar with plastic wrap and secure it with the rubber band. Make certain the plastic wrap is pulled tight. Use a small dab of glue to fasten one end of the toothpick to the center of the plastic wrap. Set the jar aside so the glue can dry.

2. When the glue is dry, place the jar on a table or other level surface. Gently blow through the straw onto the plastic wrap which is covering the jar. What happens?

   _____

3. Hold the straw close to the plastic wrap (but not touching it) and suck air up through the straw. What happens?

   _____

Evaluate:

1. When you blow on the surface of the plastic wrap, you are increasing the air pressure outside the jar and causing this air to push on the plastic wrap. Clear, sunny weather increases the air pressure outside the barometer. Would the weather forecaster say this was a period of high or low pressure? _____

   _____

2. What happens when the weather is cloudy and damp? Does the air pressure increase or decrease?_____

   _____

3. What kind of weather would you expect if the needle on a barometer falls? _____

   _____

4. What kind of weather would you expect if the needle on the barometer rises?

   _____

Windsock

Materials: A large plastic trash bag, electrical tape, a wire clothes hanger, a marker, and sharp scissors.

Procedure:

1. Form the clothes hanger into a circle with a straight handle. (See diagram at the right.)

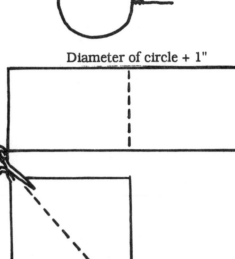

Diameter of circle + 1"

2. Measure the diameter of the circle. Cut the trash bag open along one side and the end. Spread the bag open and measure along the long side of the rectangle to one inch longer than the diameter of the clothes hanger circle. Cut off the extra plastic.

3. Fold the plastic in half and measure nine inches up from the fold on one side. Mark this spot with a marker. Cut from this spot to the unfolded corner on the opposite side.

9 in.

4. Tape the slant sides together to form an open cone shape. Overlap the seam side one inch.

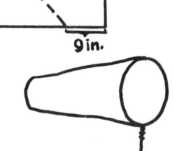

5. Tape the open cone to the clothes hanger circle. You have a windsock!

6. Take the windsock outside and poke the hanger into the ground in an open area so the wind blows into it. What happens?_____

_____

7. What happens when the wind is not blowing hard?_____

_____

8. What happens when the wind is blowing hard?_____

_____

9. What happens when the wind changes direction?_____

_____

Name _____

Anemometer

Materials: An empty, plastic, half-gallon milk jug, a thick rubber band, a three-inch square piece of cardboard, 2 three-inch nails, a marker, and scissors.

Procedure:

1. Cut a small hole (approximately the size of a dime) in the bottom of the milk jug. Cut a 3" x 5" rectangular-shaped hole in one side of the milk jug.

2. Cut a small slit in the cardboard rectangle ½ inch from each short side. Thread the rubber band through each of these slits. (See diagram.)

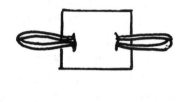

3. Place the cardboard inside the jug and pull one end of the rubber band out through the hole in the bottom of the jug. Stick a nail between the sides of the rubber band to hold it in place. (See diagram.)

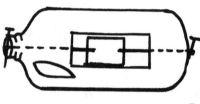

4. Stretch the rubber band up through the jug and pull the other end out through the open neck of the jug. Anchor it with the other nail. (See diagram.)

5. Slide the cardboard rectangle so that it is in the center of the opening and is parallel to the open side of the jug. (See diagram.)

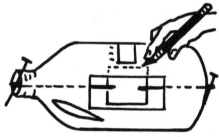

6. Turn the jug sideways and mark the spot on the side of the jug where the top of the cardboard almost touches. Label this *0*. (See diagram.)

7. Cut the scale at the bottom of this page and hold it against your jug. Wrap this scale around your jug and mark your jug to match this scale. (See diagram.)

8. Take your anemometer outdoors on a windy day and hold the jug by the handle so the wind can blow through the opening. Note the location of the edge of the cardboard. This will tell you the approximate speed of the wind.

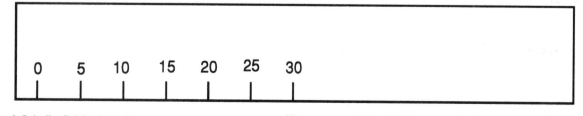

0   5   10   15   20   25   30

Seismograph

Materials: A large spring, a weight (a very large hex nut will do), a marker, a piece of paper, electrical tape, a large cardboard box, paper clips, and a ring stand.

Procedure:

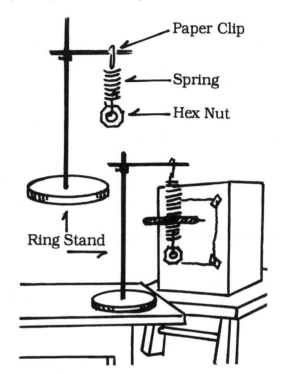

1. Use a paper clip to fasten one end of the spring to the ring stand. Use another paper clip to fasten a weight to the other end of the spring. The weight should pull the spring enough to keep it steady, so it moves slightly when the ring stand is jostled but does not bounce around wildly. Place the apparatus on a table.

2. Fasten the marker to one coil of the spring with the electrical tape.

3. Place the cardboard box so that the marker touches one side of it. Tape the paper to the box at this point.

4. Shake the table slightly. What happens? _____
   _____

5. Move the box so the pen touches a clean spot on the paper. Shake the table a little harder. What happens? _____
   _____

Evaluate:

1. What should you do if you feel the tremors of an earthquake? _____
   _____

2. What are the dangers from a severe earthquake? _____
   _____

Research: Where have the most recent earthquakes occurred in the United States? How severe were they? How much damage did they do?

Measuring Earthquakes

In 1935, Charles F. Richter created the Richter Scale to measure earthquakes. This scale assigns numbers from 0 to 8.6 to earthquakes, based on the height of the shock waves. Richter's scale is logarithmic, which means that each whole number is 10 times greater than the whole number before it. In other words, the shock waves of an earthquake which is 2.0 on the Richter Scale are 10 times higher than the waves of an earthquake which registers 1.0. In terms of danger and destruction, the actual power and force difference between the two numbers is closer to 31.5 times greater.

The 1989 earthquake near Oakland and San Francisco, California, registered 7.1 on the Richter Scale. The 1987 earthquake near Los Angeles registered 5.9 on the Richter Scale. How much greater were the shock waves of the 1989 earthquake?

_____

How much more powerful in terms of danger and destruction was the 1989 earthquake than the 1987 earthquake? _____

_____

The Richter Scale is not accurate when measuring earthquakes above 8.3. In 1977 a geophysicist named Kanamori devised the Moment Magnitude Scale. Using this scale, the Alaska earthquake of 1964 registered 9.2 M (8.4 on the Richter Scale) and was the largest recorded in North America. In 1960, the earthquake in Chile registered 9.5 M, the largest recorded anywhere in the world.

Another scale, named the Mercalli Intensity Scale, measures the intensity of the earthquake or the amount of damage the earthquake causes. This scale divides quakes into 12 levels of severity from earthquakes which are not even felt by most people (1) to earthquakes that destroy everything and even cause the earth to ripple in huge waves (12).

Research: What causes earthquakes? Can people make earthquakes?

Evaluate: Why do some severe earthquakes cause less damage than some smaller quakes? _____

Chapter Two

_____

_____

Light and Lenses

Teacher Notes

We accept Einstein's theory of the dual nature of light. We now consider light as photons of energy which act like particles at times and like waves at other times. Have students research the older theories of light such as Isaac Newton's theory of particles or "corpuscles" of light as he called them; Christian Huygen's theory of light waves; Thomas Young's theory of "interference" which supported the wave theory; and Max Planck's theory of "quanta" or small packets of energy. Also research James Clerk Maxwell, the Scottish physicist who discovered the connection between electricity and light and magnetism; Edward Morley and Albert Michelson, the American physicists who proved that luminiferous ether did not exist (nineteenth century scientists devised luminiferous ether as an invisible material which carried light through a vacuum); Philipp Lenard, the German physicist who discovered the "photo-electric effect" which occurred when light bounced electrons off certain metals.

For a bulletin board to accompany this unit, have students bring pictures of different instruments and machines which use light and lenses. Display bar codes, pictures of rainbows, and light bulbs. Discuss the many uses for light and lenses and the development of inventions such as Edison's light bulb. How does light from a candle or a light bulb differ from sunlight?

Sunlight: What Is It?

This activity is designed to help the student discover some of the properties of light. The first part covers the spectrum and the colors of the different wavelengths of light. The second part covers refraction, absorption, and the reflection of light and introduces Einstein's theory of light. Discuss the fact that an object is a certain color because of reflected light. The object absorbs all the other wavelengths of light and reflects the color which is visible to the human eye. When all of the wavelengths are absorbed we see the color black; when all are reflected the object appears white.

Interference

This activity demonstrates the way that waves interfere with one another. Water waves, air waves, and electromagnetic waves all act this way, canceling one another when the circular wave patterns intersect. The soap bubble experiment demonstrates this also. The light rays are reflected off the bubble's surface at different angles and some of the rays cross each other and leave clear spots.

Sunlight and Mirrors: The Periscope

The periscope demonstrates the reflection of light. Discuss the ways in which periscopes are used, particularly on submarines. What else could be used in place of periscopes? Why is a periscope particularly useful at times?

Bending Light

Refraction of light is a fascinating phenomenon to observe. This activity demonstrates light bending through water and through lenses. Obtain lenses from an optician and explain and demonstrate the difference between the lenses for farsightedness and near-sightedness. Diagram the passage of light through a concave lens and through a convex lens. (Enlarge the diagrams below or draw your own.)

convex lens

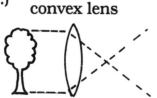

concave lens

converges light rays and makes objects seem nearer (larger)

spreads light rays and makes objects seem farther away (smaller)

The Microscope

The microscope, telescope, binoculars, and magnifying glasses all use convex lenses to enlarge the image. This activity shows how to build a simple microscope. Discuss the uses for the microscope. Introduce a commercially made laboratory microscope and explain how it works and identify its parts. Compare the high-powered electron microscopes with the small student microscopes.

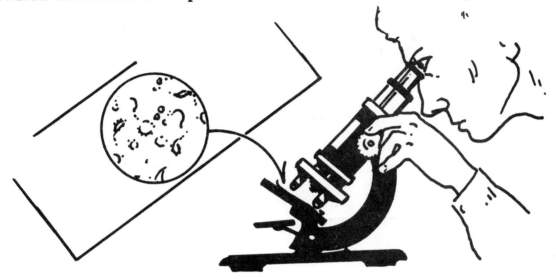

For further research, have students explore the development of the microscope. What are the advantages of the best microscopes in use today? Have students look at several different items under the microscope, such as a fungus, a hair, a piece of a butterfly wing, salt, sugar, and a drop of pond water. If you have the use of more than one kind of microscope, have students look at the items under each and compare observations. Have them compare their observations of items seen under the laboratory microscope to their observations of the same items seen under their "homemade" microscopes.

Filmstrip Projector

This activity allows students to make a working model of a filmstrip projector. A roll of medium to heavy weight acetate may be used for the film, or sheets of film for an overhead projector may be cut into strips and used as individual strips or taped together with clear tape. Students may make their own comic strips or action films by drawing directly on the film with dry markers (or any marker designed for use on acetate film).

A Zoetrope

The zoetrope was a popular toy in the 1800s and demonstrates the effect of motion produced by the rapid movement of a series of still pictures. This same effect can be produced with a stack of index cards or a small pad of paper. Draw a simple picture on each page or card in a series of gradually changing positions. Flip the stack of cards or pages of the pad to produce the effect of motion.

Lasers and Bar Codes

Lasers are not something that can be made simply and safely in the classroom. Use this sheet to stimulate discussion. How are lasers used? (for entertainment, in medicine, for industry) Particularly, what are the new medical advances which use lasers?

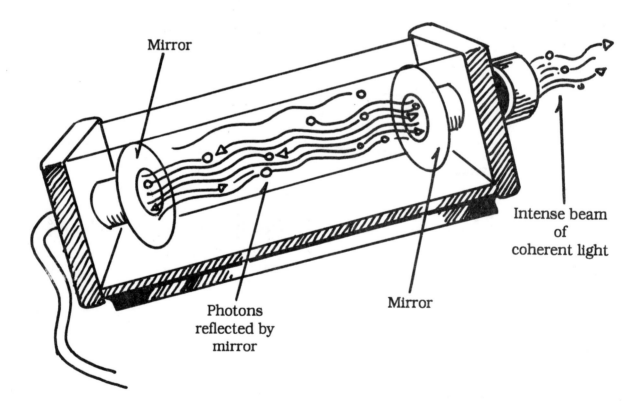

Mirror

Intense beam
of
coherent light

Photons
reflected by
mirror

Mirror

Sunlight: What Is It?

Materials: A mirror, a sunny window, an 11" x 17" sheet of white paper, white cloth, black cloth, a glass of water, a pencil, crayons or colored markers, and scissors.

Procedure:

1. Hold the white paper so the sun from the window shines on it. What color do you see on the paper? _____

   _____

2. Fold the white paper in half the long way and cut a narrow slit (1/4" wide x 3" long) one inch from one end of the paper. See the diagram at the right. Open the paper and fold it sideways so the top of the paper is just above the rim of the glass. Place the glass of water in front of the slit so that sunlight from the window shines through the slit and through the glass onto the paper and forms a rainbow or spectrum of light. Move the glass and paper to get the clearest and brightest spectrum. What colors do you see on the paper?

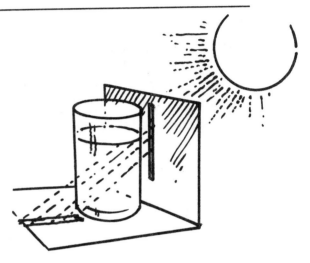

   _____

   _____

   _____

Light is part of the spectrum of electromagnetic waves. The diagram below illustrates the entire spectrum.

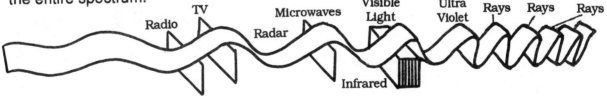

Different colors of light travel at different speeds. Red is the slowest and violet is the fastest. Color the band below in the correct colors, starting with red on the left. Use the spectrum you saw through your glass as a guide.

3. Place one end of a pencil in the water in the glass. Observe closely. What seems to happen to the pencil as it enters the water?_____

_____

_____

Light travels more quickly through air than through water which causes this effect.

4. Light can be reflected or absorbed. Place the white cloth over your bare arm and hold it in the sunlight. How does your arm feel? _____

_____

5. Place the black cloth over your arm and hold it in the sunlight. How does your arm feel? _____

_____

6. Which color absorbs the sunlight? _____

7. Which color reflects the sunlight?_____

8. Hold a mirror in the sunlight for just a second. DO NOT HOLD IT SO THAT IT SHINES LIGHT IN SOMEONE'S EYES. DO NOT HOLD IT IN THE SUN FOR A LONG TIME. What happens? _____

_____

9. Even a mirror absorbs *some* light, but it does reflect most of it. Have you ever stood between two parallel full-length mirrors? If you look in one, you see many reflections of yourself. If you look carefully, you see that at one point the reflections fade because there is not enough reflected light to be visible. If you have two full-length parallel mirrors, stand between them and count the number of images of yourself you see on one side. At what point does the image fade? _____

_____

10. Einstein theorized that light is made of little packets of energy, which we now call **photons**. Sometimes light acts like waves and sometimes like particles. As a wave, it travels through substances like air and water. Thump against your chair with the palm of your hand. Can you feel the vibrations?_____

_____

Light travels through substances this way, in vibrating waves. Light also acts like a particle. Light could not travel as a wave in outer space where there is no matter. There it travels like a particle, like a tiny ball hurtling through the blank space.

Interference

Materials: A large flat pan half full of water, a small pebble, a flashlight, scissors, black construction paper, a movie screen, tape, a bucket half full of water, one bottle of dishwashing liquid, ¼ cup of sugar, and several pieces of bendable wire at least a foot in length.

Procedure:

1. When the water is still, gently drop the pebble into the center of the pan. Draw the pattern of the ripples formed by the pebble in the space below.

Light waves spread out from their source in circles just like waves or ripples in a pond.

2. From the black paper, cut a circle that is just slightly larger than the end of the flashlight. Cut two parallel slits in the center of the circle. The slits should be ⅛" wide and 1" long. Space them ½" apart. Tape the black paper over the end of the flashlight. See the diagram below for assistance.

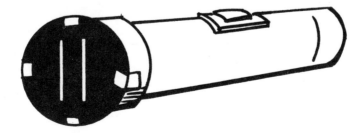

3. Darken the room and shine the flashlight on the movie screen. Draw the pattern of light that you see in the space below.

The pattern you saw is caused by refraction. A beam of light comes out of each slit in the paper. When the two circles of light cross each other they cancel each other, forming dark spots. This also happens with colored bands of light.

4. Mix the bottle of dishwashing liquid and the sugar with the water in the bucket.

5. Bend the wire into shapes. Make at least one flat shape and at least one three-dimensional shape (see the diagram below).

6. Dip the shapes into the liquid to form soap bubbles. Do not blow these bubbles off the shapes. Instead, carry them on the wire to a sunny window and observe the colors.

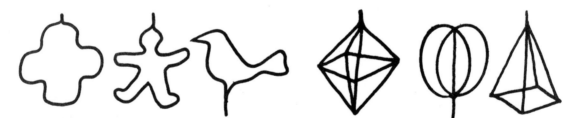

What is the difference between the colors on the flat shapes and the colors on the three-dimensional shapes? _____

_____

7. Can you see any places where the colored bands cancel each other and the colors disappear? _____

_____

— Sunlight and Mirrors: The Periscope —

One way of using the reflecting power of mirrors and light is the periscope. Since the human eyeball cannot bend around corners or extend upward or outward, the periscope can be a very useful item.

Materials: Two rectangular mirrors each 1½" x 3", gift box cardboard or posterboard, glue, masking tape, and scissors.

Note: If you do not have mirrors exactly this size, make the following adjustments. For a slightly smaller mirror, mount it on one end of a 1½" x 3" piece of posterboard. For a slightly larger mirror, change the slits as directed in step one. Use the diagram below as a guide.

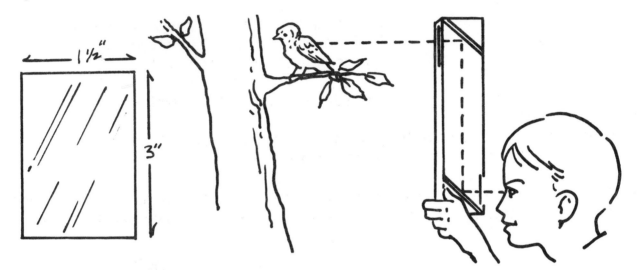

Procedure:

1. Glue the pattern on the following page onto an 8½" x 11" piece of posterboard or cardboard. When the glue is dry, cut out the pattern following the heavy black lines. Cut slits where the pattern says "slits." Do not cut beyond the solid lines if your mirrors are 1½" x 3" or smaller. If your mirrors are larger, cut the shaded portion also. Cut the two peepholes, one at the top and one at the bottom, where the pattern says "eye hole."

2. Fold the pattern on the dotted lines to form a long, slender rectangle. Tape the sides together where the pattern says "tape."

3. Insert the mirrors into the slits. The mirrors should face each other at angles. Look through one of the peepholes. What do you see? _____

_____

Name ____________________

Periscope Pattern

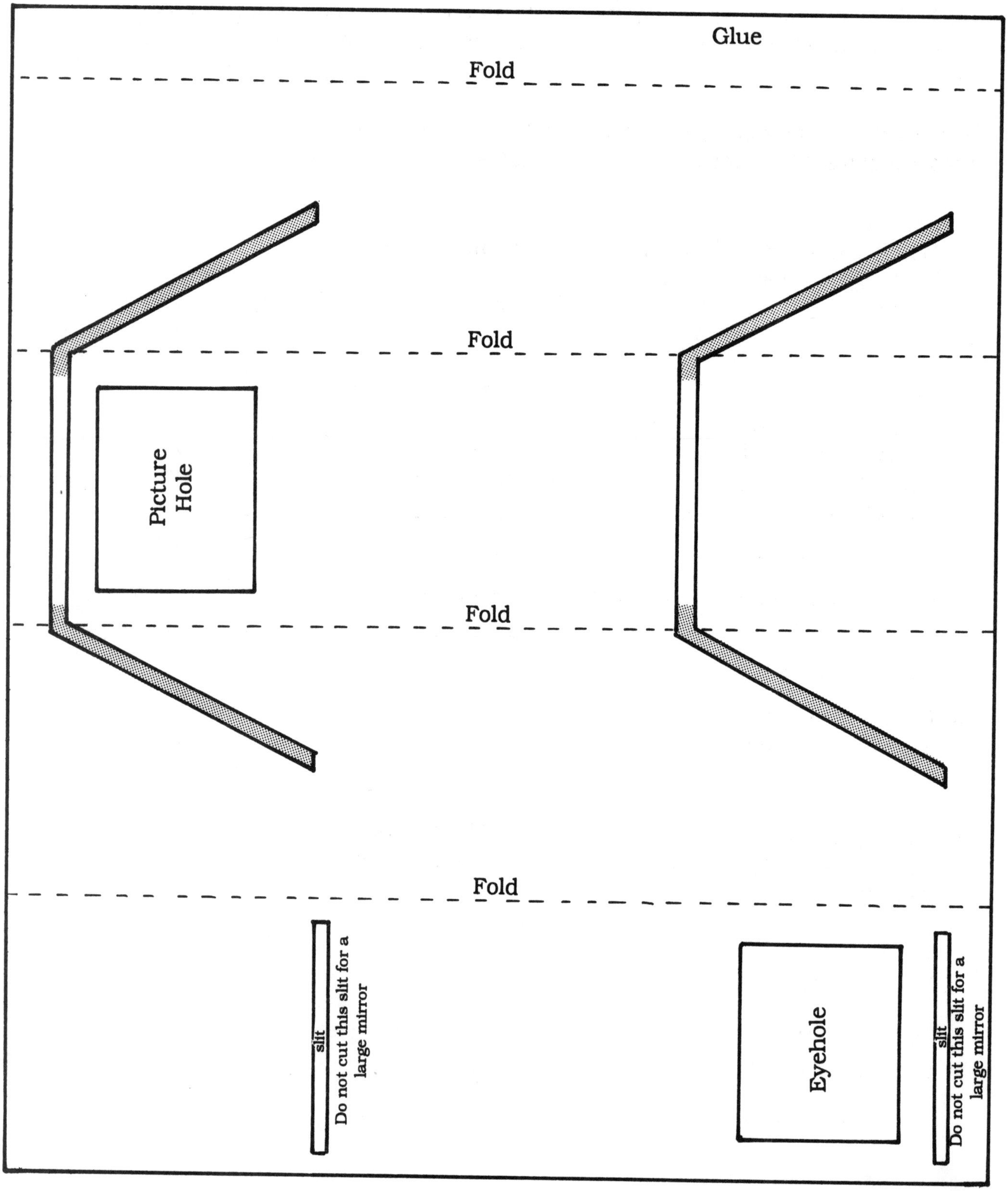
Glue
Fold
Fold
Picture Hole
Fold
Fold
slit
Do not cut this slit for a large mirror
Eyehole
slit
Do not cut this slit for a large mirror

Bending Light

The bending of light is called *refraction*. Light is bent when it goes through water (this is what causes a pencil in a glass of water to look bent) and when it goes through a curved glass lens.

Materials: An index card, a flashlight, a clear glass full of water, a convex lens (magnifying glass), a concave lens, and scissors.

Procedure:

1. Cut slits in one index card about ⅟₃₂" wide and ¼" apart as in the diagram to the right. Leave a ¾" solid border around the card so that you can hold it stiff.

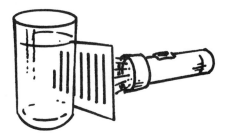

2. Darken the room. Hold the index card behind the glass full of water. Shine the flashlight through the holes in the card and through the water in the glass as in the diagram. What happens to the rays of light? _____

_____

3. Replace the glass of water with the convex lens and repeat the experiment. What happens to the rays of light? _____

_____

4. Replace the convex lens with the concave lens and repeat the experiment. What happens to the rays of light? _____

_____

5. This bending of light through lenses is used for several different instruments, especially for the telescope, binoculars, and the microscope. What are some other uses for lenses? _____

_____

6. When you look through a convex lens, what happens to the image you are seeing?

_____

7. When you look through a concave lens, what happens to the image you are seeing?

_____

The Microscope

Materials: A magnifying glass, a paper towel tube, scissors, a three-inch square piece of posterboard or cardboard, a convex lens, and several very small objects.

Procedure:

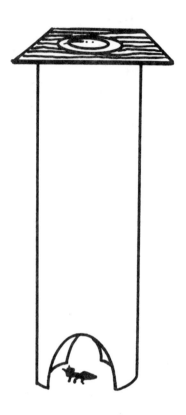

1. Hold the convex lens above the object you want to see so that the image is sharp and in focus. Measure the distance from the object to the lens. Cut the paper towel tube this length. Cut out the sides of the tube part way up to form two thick legs that let light in on each side. Use the diagram at the side for a guide.

2. In the center of the square posterboard, cut out a circle slightly smaller than the convex lens, so that the lens can fit in the circle without slipping through it.

3. Place the object you want to see under this tube apparatus. Make certain light shines through the sides so that the object is clearly visible.

4. Hold the magnifying glass above the convex lens. Move the magnifying glass until the object under the lens is clearly visible and in sharp focus. You have made a microscope. What do you see?

_____

_____

Observe several different objects. Make drawings of your observations below. Label your drawings.

Filmstrip Projector

Materials: Acetate film, scissors, a ruler, permanent markers, a shoebox, two 12-inch pieces of ¼" dowel, Scotch tape, and a flashlight that is at least 1½ inches shorter than the shoebox.

Procedure:

1. Cut a long strip of acetate two inches wide. Use a marker to draw lines across the strip every two inches. This will give you a string of two-inch boxes. Draw a story in these boxes with markers. You can make one figure that changes position slightly in each box for a moving picture effect or separate pictures that tell a story for a filmstrip still-picture effect.

2. Cut a two-inch square opening in one end of the shoebox.

3. Make two holes on each side of the shoe box. The holes should be ½" from each end of the box and one inch down from the top. These holes are for the dowels. Fit a dowel through each set of holes as in the illustration.

4. Make a 2½" slit on each end of the bottom of the box ½" from each end.

5. Tape the beginning end of your film to the dowel near the two-inch square opening. Thread the rest of the film through the slit under that dowel, under the shoebox, and through the back slit. Wind the extra film around the back dowel inside the shoebox.

6. Tape the flashlight inside the shoebox so that the film can slide freely and the light shines through the opening.

7. Darken the room and shine your projector on a white wall, a screen, or a sheet of white paper.

8. Roll your film up on the front dowel. Roll it quickly for moving pictures.

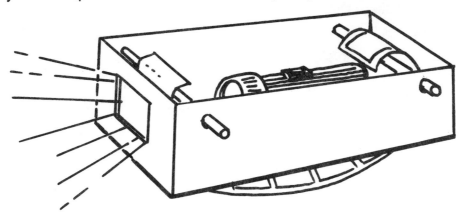

A Zoetrope

Cameras, movies, and videos all use light and lenses. In addition, movies use a trick of the vision. A movie is a series of still pictures which are moved quickly to produce the effect of motion. The brain interprets this series of quickly changing pictures as one picture which is moving. The zoetrope was a popular toy invented in the 1800s and uses moving pictures to produce the effect of motion.

Materials: A block of wood, an empty thread spool, a long nail, a hammer, an empty margarine or whipped topping container, sharp scissors, a sheet of white paper, and an 8" x 12" rectangle of posterboard.

Procedure:
1. Cut slits in the margarine container 2" long x ¼" wide. Space these slits evenly around the container. The slits should be two inches apart. (See diagram to the right.)
2. Make a small hole in the exact center of the container. The hole should be just large enough to let the nail move in and out smoothly.
3. Place the spool on top of the block of wood and the container on top of the spool. Nail the container through the hole in the spool to the block. (See diagram.)
4. Fold the posterboard on each side to make it stand up around the container as in the diagram. Cut a small hole to see through. The top of the hole should be even with the top of the container and the bottom of the hole should be even with the bottom of the slits.
5. Cut out the strips on the next page. Fit one inside the bottom of the container with the pictures facing inward. (See diagram.)
6. Look through the viewing hole while you spin the container very rapidly. What happens?

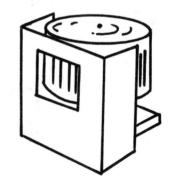

_____

_____

7. Use these strips or make your own to make your own "home movies."

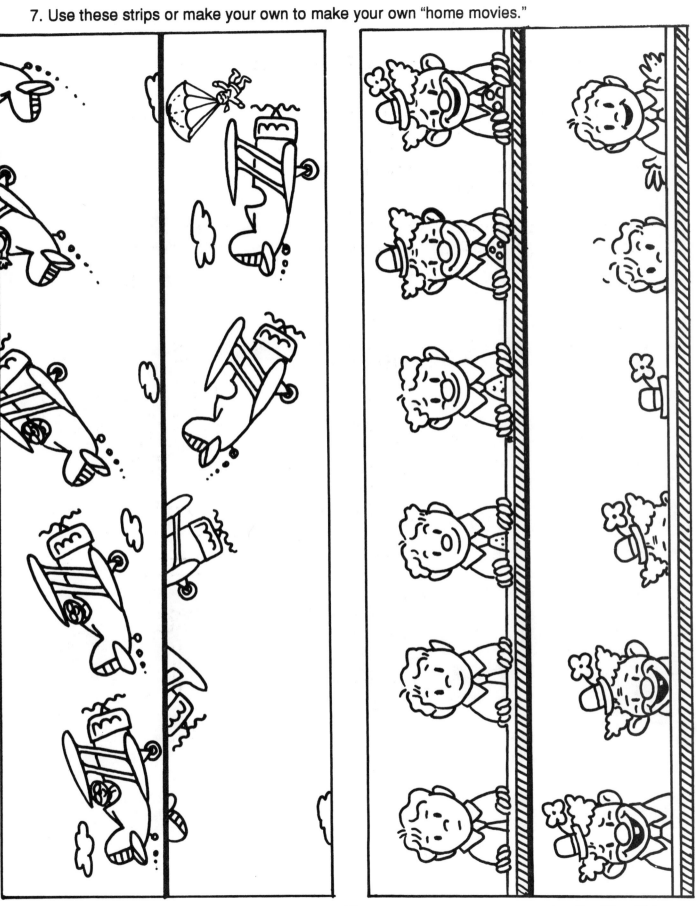

Lasers and Bar Codes

Ordinary light is made up of waves of light that are different lengths. Red light waves are slow and far apart, purple light waves are fastest and closest together. Laser light is made of pure light beams that are all the same length. Compare the two diagrams below. Coloring the bands of ordinary light will make the diagram even easier to understand. The colors are listed next to the correct band.

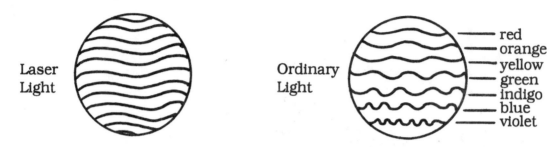

Laser
Light

Ordinary
Light

——— red
——— orange
——— yellow
——— green
——— indigo
——— blue
——— violet

A laser consists of a tube containing a mixture of gases such as helium and neon or a crystal such as a ruby, an electrical power source, and a reflective resonator (usually parallel mirrors at either end of the tube). The electricity excites the substance or substances in the tube, causing them to emit photons of light energy. The light waves bounce around in the tube exciting other atoms and producing more light. The light is bounced back and forth off the two mirrors, and only the photons of the same phase, direction, and wavelength keep bouncing. When the number of photons accumulates to a certain level, some exit the tube through a partially reflecting mirror. They are seen as a very intense, continuous beam of light. LASER stands for Light Amplification by Stimulated Emission of Radiation. See the diagram below.

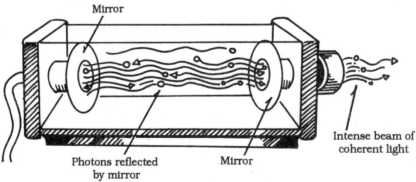

Mirror

Photons reflected
by mirror

Mirror

Intense beam of
coherent light

Laser beams are useful for such things as bar code scanners. A laser beam reflects the image of the bar code to a photodetector. The intensity of the laser beam varies with the width of the bands and whether they are black or white. These signals are converted to electrical current in a pattern that corresponds to the UPC number. The store's computer interprets these electrical impulses and translates them into the correct description and price of the item.

Collect bar codes from several different items and compare them. Describe your findings.

Chapter Three

Harnessing Energy

———— Teacher Notes ————

We use the energy from the sun for heat, for solar cells, and for light. We use chemical energy to power motors and engines and to produce electricity. We use wind energy to power sailboats and windmills and water power to generate electricity. This chapter demonstrates some of the machines we have developed to harness different forms of energy and gives students an opportunity to develop their own scientific creativity by designing some machines which use the more available and less commonly used forms of energy—water and wind.

Windmill Rider

The windmill first came into use in Persia in the seventh century. Windmills are associated with Holland, where they were used widely during the 1700s to pump water from the lowlands. Many windmills are still used for pumping water and milling grain in the countries which border the Mediterranean. In the United States, windmills were built for these purposes in the 1800s and early 1900s. Windmills are being revived as a means of producing electricity. In California, wind "farms" use windmills to drive generators to produce electricity. This activity demonstrates the principles of the windmill and the gear system which translates wind power into circular movement for grinding or pumping. It also allows students to build a small toy moved by wind power.

Windmills, Turbines, and Dentist Drills

Windmills are not extinct; they have just been put to different uses. *National Geographic*, December 1975, contained an excellent article on some more recent windmill designs and uses. This activity sheet covers some of the uses for the windmill and the types of windmill sails still commonly in use on conventional windmills. Encourage creativity on the last question of this activity, which asks students to consider other uses for the windmill. Could a person make a windmill-powered car? Heat a house?

Water Power

The water wheel was more common in early America than the windmill. Many old water wheels are still in existence; some are still in use. Engineers and inventors are experimenting with modern designs to make use of our many creeks and rivers and ocean currents. A small creek with a steady flow can produce enough electrical power for one household. Drought is a major hindrance to popularizing individual hydroelectric generators just as the fickleness of the wind hampers wind turbines in most areas of the world. How could we solve these problems? Could we devise a convertible design or a design which utilizes both options? Could we combine them with solar power?

Sun-Cooked S'mores

Anyone who has experienced a sunburn has some idea of the heat and power of the sun. This activity angles the sun's rays to produce a cooker. A round-shaped cooker would also be effective. If you have access to a bowl with a round bottom (the interior surface must be totally rounded with no flat surfaces; wooden bowls sometimes have totally round bottoms in the interior), cover the inside with foil and angle it toward the sun. Would a triangular, prism shape work? Cut three identical triangles, cover them with foil, and tape them together. Compare the designs. Which works best? Why do these cookers work? Diagram the direction of the sun's rays as they strike the foil and are reflected.

Solar Power

Solar cells are most practical for space satellites because in space there is no atmosphere and no cloud cover to block the sun's rays. However, solar-powered vehicles have also been designed and tested. *National Geographic*, November 1983, contained an excellent article on one solar-powered vehicle named The Quiet Achiever, which was designed by Hans Tholstrup and Larry Perkins. The vehicle weighed 276 pounds and had a cruising speed of 15 miles per hour (its top speed was approximately 39 miles per hour). The vehicle crossed the continent of Australia in 20 days. In 1981, the *Solar Challenger*, a solar-powered aircraft, crossed the English Channel.

Discuss other uses for solar power. Have students research solar heating systems. Discuss ways to build solar-heated houses and ways to modify older houses to make better use of solar power. Have a house design competition to see who can come up with the best ways to use solar power and conserve energy. What can we do to increase use of sun power and decrease our dependence on other sources of energy?

Chemical Energy

This experiment demonstrates the release of chemical energy from an exothermic chemical reaction. Oxidation of the steel wool produces **heat energy.** Encourage use of this term. Students may need guidance to reach this conclusion in the evaluation section of this activity. Explain that the warmth which causes the temperature to rise in the jar is heat energy and that it is a result of the chemical reaction between the steel wool and the oxygen in the air.

Discuss the many uses for chemical energy, such as powering vehicles, heating homes and offices, generating electricity, and cooking food. Ask students for concrete examples of ways we use chemical energy. How is this a problem for us in terms of natural resources such as gasoline, coal, oil, and trees? Could we make more efficient use of these natural resources?

Combustion Engine

There are two basic types of combustion engines, **internal combustion engines** and **external combustion engines.** This activity introduces both types and demonstrates the movement of the piston. Give students examples of combustion engines and ask them to identify which are external and which are internal combustion engines. For instance, lawnmowers, cars, trucks, tractors, airplanes, and helicopters all have internal combustion engines. Old-fashioned steamboats and steam locomotives used external combustion engines. Use this diagram to differentiate between the two types.

Internal Combustion Engine

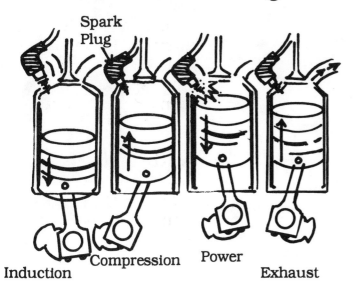

Spark Plug

Induction Compression Power Exhaust

External Combustion Engine

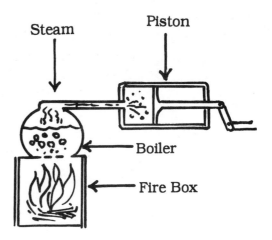

Steam Piston

Boiler

Fire Box

For a bulletin board, provide or have students bring pictures of different machines which are powered by external and internal combustion engines. Classify and, if possible, label them as gasoline, diesel, or jet engines. Use this display as an illustration for students' reports on these topics.

Motors

This experiment demonstrates the principles behind electric motors. The activity sheet also explains the difference between induction motors (the name comes from the fact that the current flowing through the stator induces a current in the rotor) and the universal motor (this motor is universal because it can use either alternating or direct current). Explain these terms and the terms **stator,** which refers to the stationary coil, and **rotor,** which refers to the rotating coil, before you start this activity. After students have completed the activity, ask: In this experiment, which part is the stator? (The coil of wire is the stator.) Which part is the rotor? (The magnet on the string is the rotor.)

Below are diagrams of the universal motor and the induction motor.

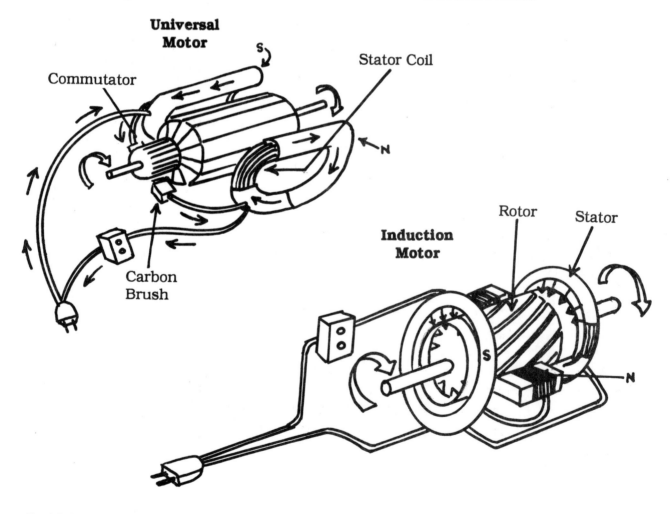

Windmill Rider

The first windmills were built in Persia about 1300 years ago. Windmills use wind power to grind grain or pump water. Windmills are still used in the countries that border the Mediterranean Sea.

A windmill is very similar to a large pinwheel. The wind turns the sails and the sails turn a central shaft attached to a series of gears.

Materials: A six-inch piece of ¼" dowel, two thumbtacks, a toilet paper tube, a three-ounce plastic or paper drinking cup, a straight pin, pliers, two 6" pieces of yarn, scissors, posterboard, and Elmer's glue.

Procedure:

1. Cut out the patterns at the bottom of the next page and trace each pattern onto the posterboard. Cut out each pattern carefully, keeping each notch, cutting only on the solid lines.

2. Push the point of a thumbtack through the square at each dot, starting with the dot numbered "1." Bend the flaps of the square as you go to form the pinwheel shape shown in the diagram to the right. These are the sails.

3. Push the point of the thumbtack through the center of the flat part of one end of the dowel. Make certain it is stuck tight.

4. Cut two smooth, semicircular notches at one end of the toilet paper tube so the dowel can move freely and evenly in the notches. See the diagram to the right.

5. Stick gear A to the other end of the dowel with the second thumbtack.

6. Poke the point of the straight pin through the center of the bottom of the drinking cup so the point is sticking out of the cup as in the diagram to the right. Stick this point through the center hole of gear B.

7. Place the drinking cup near the toilet paper tube so the notches in gears A and B fit together and gear A can turn gear B.

8. Punch holes at the dots marked on the bug figure. Thread one piece of yarn through the top hole and tie it to form a handle loop.

9. Punch a hole through the center of gear C. Thread the second piece of yarn through this hole and through the bottom hole of the bug figure to make the legs of the figure riding a unicycle. Tie the yarn. Fit the notches of gear C into the notches of gear B. Hold the bug figure up so the unicycle wheel notches just fit into gear B. Have a friend blow hard on the windmill sails. What happens?

_____

_____

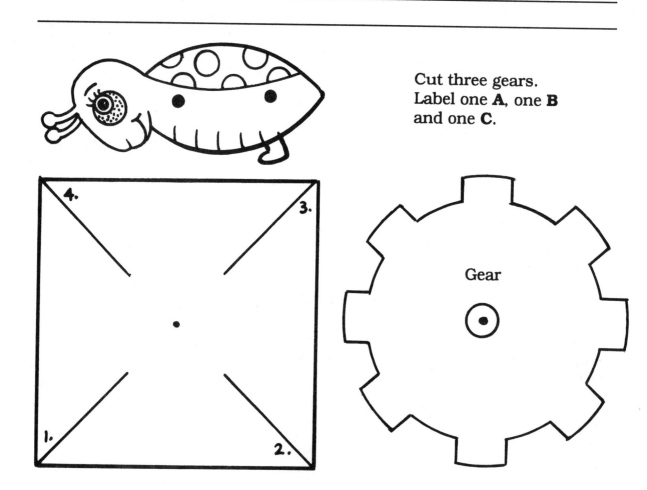

Cut three gears. Label one **A**, one **B** and one **C**.

Gear

— Windmills, Turbines, and Dentist Drills —

What do these all have in common? They are all variations of the windmill. Old-fashioned windmills were used for grinding grain or pumping water. In some places in the world this type of windmill is still in use. We tend to think of Holland as the land of windmills, but actually many windmills in use today can be found in Portugal, Spain, and Turkey. The sails are made of cloth or wood and are of two basic types.

1. The **jib sail** is triangular and made of cloth. When the wind is strong, the miller folds or furls up the sail. When the wind is weak, he unfolds the cloth to make the sail larger. Why does he need to do this? Why would he not leave the sail the same size all the time?

_____

2. The **spring sail** is rectangular in shape and made of wooden shutters. The shutters turn against a spring and open when the wind is blowing hard. When the wind slows, the spring pushes the shutters closed again. This type of windmill sail was invented in the eighteenth century. Why is this type easier for the millers than the jib-sail windmills?

_____

3. Modern windmills are used to power a generator converting wind energy into electricity. The blades of these windmills are made like airplane wings. They turn very swiftly and have gears designed to make the drive shaft turn even more quickly. A computer controls a special mounting assembly which turns the windmill so it is constantly facing into the wind. Why does the windmill need to face the wind?

_____

4. Did you know your dentist's drill is a miniature windmill? The windmill is on its side and the air is forced against it like a waterwheel. The windmill turns the shaft of the drill and the drill bit turns very rapidly and makes a neat little hole in your tooth.

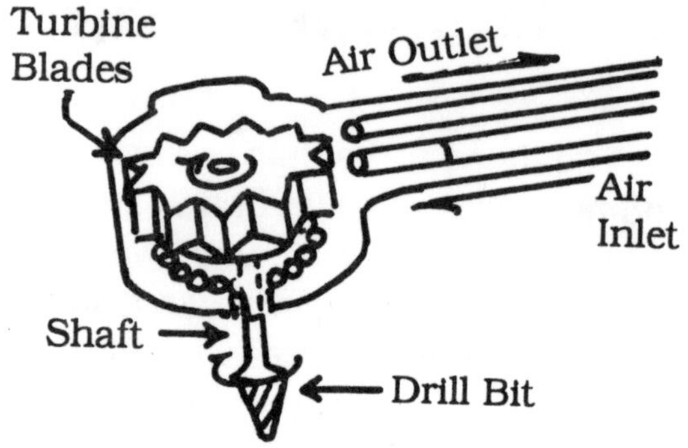

Turbine Blades

Air Outlet

Air Inlet

Shaft →

← Drill Bit

5. What other things could you do with a windmill? Can you think up some inventions that could use wind power? Use the space below to draw or tell about your ideas.

Water Power

Water wheels are very similar to windmills. They were in use in Greece in the first century B.C. This early Greek water wheel was horizontal. Water flowed down a chute and hit against the paddles, turning the wheel and the central axle.

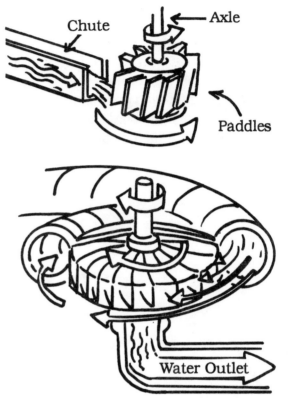

The modern hydroelectric turbine uses this same horizontal water wheel. The water flows in through pipes and strikes against carefully constructed turbine blades. The turning of these blades turns the generator shaft which powers the generator and produces electricity.

Materials: Plastic milk jugs or margarine or whipped topping containers, scissors, electrical tape, a pencil, and water.

Procedure:

1. Use the pattern on the next page to cut eight paddles and one central wheel hub from the sides of the plastic milk jug or the bottom or top of the containers. Notch the hub in the places indicated by the dark lines. Cut only on the dark lines.

2. Cut a hole in the center of the hub that will just fit the pencil. The hub should hug the pencil tightly and not slide up and down. Use electrical tape to fasten the hub to the pencil.

3. Fit the paddles on the hub as shown in the diagram to the right. Use a small piece of tape to hold the paddles in place.

4. Suspend the waterwheel over a margarine or whipped topping container. Pour water on the top of the wheel so it strikes the paddles. What happens?

_____

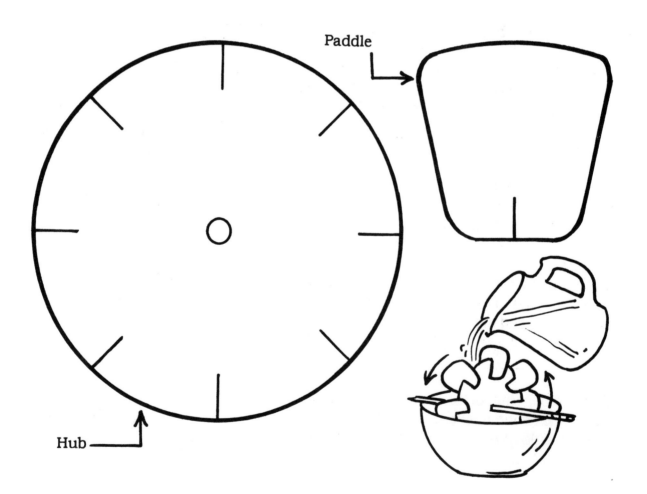

Paddle

Hub

Sun-Cooked S'mores

The energy which comes to us from the sun is much more powerful than we sometimes realize. We feel the sun's warmth and watch plants respond to the sunlight. We stay out in the sun too long and feel the effects of sunburn. Could we harness this energy to actually cook food?

Materials: Posterboard, aluminum foil, play dough or modeling clay, double-sided tape, string, scissors, marshmallows, Hershey's milk-chocolate bars, graham crackers, and skewers.

Procedure:

1. Cut a 14" square of posterboard. Cover one side of it with aluminum foil. Attach the foil with the double-sided tape and make the foil as smooth as possible. Use several small pieces of tape to attach the foil instead of long strips. Make certain that there are no gaps of exposed posterboard if you have a seam.

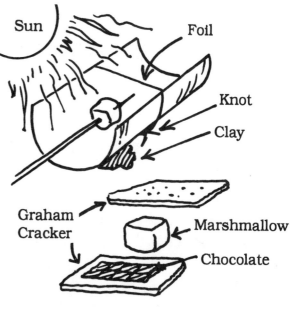

2. Bend the posterboard in a semicircular curve with the foil side in. Tie a piece of string around the outside of the cardboard to hold the curve in place. Tie a knot on the back side to hold the string tight and slide the string so it is in the center of the shape. (See the diagram to the right.)

3. Face the cooker to the sun and prop it up so the sun's rays hit the center of the foil. Use the play dough or modeling clay to make a base to help hold your cooker in place.

4. Skewer a marshmallow. Feel with your hand near the center of the cooker just above the foil until you find the hot spot. Remove your hand immediately and hold the marshmallow in that spot. What happens?

_____

5. To make s'mores, place a square (at least 1") of chocolate on one half of a graham cracker. As soon as it is cooked, place the hot marshmallow on top of the chocolate, cover it with the other half of the graham cracker, and enjoy!

Solar Power

The sun's energy can provide more than heat and light. Solar cells convert the sun's energy into electricity. Satellites orbiting the earth are powered by huge panels of solar cells. Several solar-powered cars have been designed and built. Calculators and small mechanical devices use solar cells. Why is solar power more practical for space vehicles and machines than large earth vehicles and machines? (Hint: Think of clouds.) _____

_____

How does a solar cell work? It does not have any moving mechanical parts. It is similar to a battery.

Each cell is made of two layers of silicon. The top layer of silicon is negatively charged; that is, the atoms contain extra electrons. The lower layer is positively charged. This layer is short of electrons.

When the sunlight strikes the solar cell, the electrons are released from the top layer and flow to the bottom layer, creating a current.

The current carries the electrons back to the top layer and the process starts all over again.

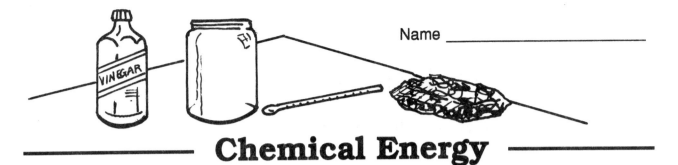

Name _____

Chemical Energy

Chemical energy is the energy which is released from a chemical reaction. When you burn something, for example, a chemical reaction takes place and the item which is burned turns to a black lump of carbon or other elements. The heat which comes from the burning is a form of chemical energy. Sometimes the chemical reaction produces a burst of force or an explosion.

Materials: A thermometer, a glass jar large enough for the thermometer to fit in, steel wool (without soap), and vinegar.

Procedure:

1. Pull off a piece of steel wool approximately an inch wide. Pull the steel wool out to make a flat, loose mat and soak it with vinegar.

2. Place the vinegar-soaked steel wool in the bottom of the glass jar. Stick the bulb end of the thermometer on top of the steel wool and screw the lid on the jar.

3. Set the jar aside. Check it every 15 minutes for two hours. Record your results on the chart below.

TIME	TEMPERATURE	OBSERVATIONS

Evaluate: When steel wool oxidizes (rusts), chemical energy is produced. How can you tell this? What form does this energy take? _____

© Frank Schaffer Publications, Inc.   41   FS-10169 Science and Technology: How Things Work

Combustion Engine

The combustion engine is an example of a machine powered by chemical energy. Automobiles use combustion engines as do airplanes, ships, motorcycles, power lawnmowers, and a number of other devices. Gasoline engines, diesel engines, steam engines, and jet engines all use combustion for power. Combustion engines are classified as one of two types—internal or external combustion engines. Internal combustion engines such as gasoline and jet engines are powered by burning the fuel inside the engine. External combustion engines such as steam engines are powered by fuel burned outside the engine. How does a combustion engine work?

Materials: A soda straw, a toilet paper tube, a plastic container lid, paper fasteners, scissors, posterboard, a pencil, a balloon, masking tape, and a three-ounce paper cup.

Procedure:

1. From the plastic container lid, cut a disc that will just fit inside of the toilet paper tube. Tape the soda straw to this disc.

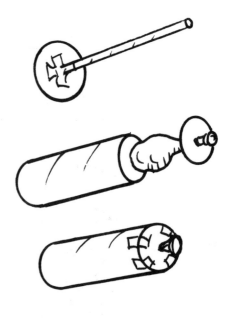

2. Out of posterboard, cut a second disc that will just cover one end of the tube. Cut a small hole in the center of this disc and fit the end of the balloon through it. Tape this disc to the tube with the open end of the balloon sticking out so you can inflate the balloon.

3. Cut out the pattern pieces below and trace them onto posterboard. Cut out the pieces and fasten them with paper fasteners as shown in the diagram to the right. Tape the straight piece to the soda straw and hook the feet of the bird over the drinking cup.

Paper Fastener

4. Inflate the balloon. What happens? _____

_____

Evaluate:

In a combustion engine, the combustion or burning takes place inside the cylinder of the piston. This is represented by the balloon in this experiment. When the force of combustion (expanding balloon) presses on the piston, what happens? _____

_____

Research: How are gasoline engines, diesel engines, and jet engines different? Use your library resources to find out about these engines and compare the way they work.

Motors

What is the difference between an engine and a motor?
How does a motor work?

The terms **motor** and **engine** are often used interchangeably. Technically an engine is any device with moving parts and a motor is anything that causes motion, or a small engine. In this activity, we use the term **motor** for the device which is powered by electricity, where engines are powered by chemical energy or some other form of energy. The motor uses an electromagnet to convert electricity to movement.

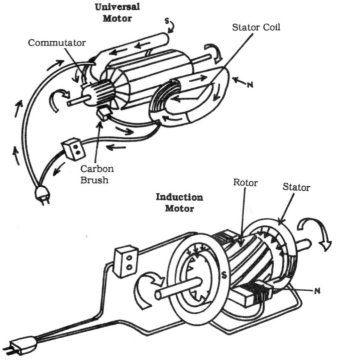

Most power tools use the universal motor. The universal motor will work with either alternating (AC) or direct current (DC). It has strong **torque** or twisting force. The universal motor consists of two stationary coils of wire and a rotor. Current flows through the coils of wire, creating an electromagnet. The rotor is also wound with coils of wire and it rubs against the wire brushes of the commutator to create a second electromagnet. The poles in this electromagnet shift alternately.

The induction motor operates only on alternating current. The current flows through the stationary coils (stator) setting up a strong magnetic field. This creates or **induces** a current in the rotor. The rotor then turns to align itself with the poles of the stator. As it does this, the current shifts in the stator.

Materials: A "C" battery, one yard of insulated copper wire, a large steel nail, a 12" piece of string, and a bar magnet.

Procedure:

1. Remove the insulation from one inch of each end of the wire. Wind the wire tightly around the nail, leaving four inches at each end. Bend each end to make a flat loop and hold one loop to each terminal of the battery. (See the diagram at the right for assistance.)

2. Have an assistant tie the string around the middle of the magnet and suspend the magnet over the wire coil. What happens?

_____

3. Have the assistant continue to hold the magnet over the coil and place the wire loops on the opposite terminals of the battery. What happens?

_____

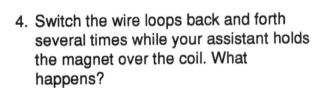

4. Switch the wire loops back and forth several times while your assistant holds the magnet over the coil. What happens?

_____

Evaluate:

1. When you change the direction of the current in an electromagnet, what happens to its magnetic poles?_____

_____

2. When the current changes direction in one of the stationary electromagnets of a motor, what happens to the moveable electromagnet? _____

_____

Chapter Four

Engineering and Physics

Teacher Notes

Engineers and physicists have developed hundreds of fascinating machines and structures using basic scientific principles. This chapter explores and explains a few of them—bridges, buildings, pumps, levers, and brakes.

Bridge Building

This experiment is concerned with the relative strength of different column shapes. The design of a bridge's supports or a building's frame dictates the strength and longevity of the bridge or building. The strength of a column increases as its weight is spread out away from its axis or center line. A circular-shaped hollow column is the strongest hollow column because all of its weight is equidistant from the center line. This activity demonstrates this fact. The fourth type of column, which is not included on the student's activity sheet, is the "I" shape. Steel columns are frequently made in this shape. To demonstrate the strength of this column, have students cut a strip of construction paper into four equal strips lengthwise. Fold ½" of both sides of each strip up to make a shape like this: [. Press down on one of these columns. It is very flimsy. Glue a pair of these shapes back to back to form an "I" shape. Test the strength of this new column shape. It is much stronger.

Collect pictures of bridges for a bulletin board to go with these activities. Study some of the bridge designs. Which designs are best for wide spans? Which work well for narrow spans? Which are most durable? Which are easiest to maintain? Discuss the problems of expansion, varying loads, corrosion, and wind. (The Tacoma Narrows Bridge collapsed in 1940, four months after it was built, because of high winds. The wind caused the bridge to sway and twist and literally twisted it apart.) What are good materials for bridge building? Have students research and write a short report on some of the more famous bridges and bridge designs. Some suggestions are the Roman arch, the Sydney Harbor Bridge and the Gladesville Bridge in Australia, the Brooklyn Bridge, and the New River Gorge Bridge in West Virginia.

Suspension Bridges

A suspension bridge must be anchored at both ends. The cables cannot simply be strung between the towers. They must be anchored in the ground on either side. If they are not anchored, the weight of the bridge and anything that is on it will pull the towers inward. To demonstrate this, have students put one hand on top of their heads and pull on their heads. Do you feel the pull on your neck? Does it tend to bend in the direction your hand is pulling? Instruct students to put both hands on top of their heads and pull equally with both hands. Is it easier to keep your head straight this way?

Building Buildings

One structure can be made out of the same materials as another structure but be much stronger, simply because the materials are formed into a different shape. Building trusses for houses are triangular with reinforcements on the interior to keep the legs of the triangle together. This experiment compares different truss designs and allows students to test each kind.

Shape and Strength

Shape alone affects the strength of a material. This experiment demonstrates how changing shape changes the strength of paper. A flat piece of paper provides little support, but the ridges and folds of different shapes give strength. Have students research different building designs and collect pictures of different designs. Which one would support heavy snowfalls? Which ones can accommodate large crowds of people and heavy weights in their interior? Which designs are most flexible and will withstand earthquakes?

A Pump

How does a hand pump draw water up from a well or force air into a tire? This experiment shows how the suction of the piston pulls air or water into the interior of the cylinder and forces it out the outlet.

Levers

We use levers in so many devices that we tend to take them for granted. This activity defines the three basic types of levers and demonstrates the differences between them. Encourage use of the terms **fulcrum, load,** and **effort.** The three types of levers are:

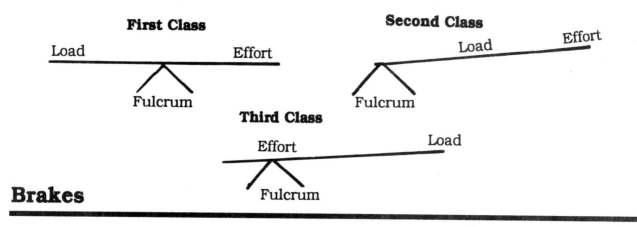

Brakes

This activity explains two basic types of brakes. Both kinds of brakes work because of friction. The disc brakes on a car lock the wheels so they drag against the road and the friction stops the car. Compare these to bicycle brakes which also lock the tire. The bobsled brakes are more like the teeth on figure skates.

Moving Heavy Things

Wheels make even the heaviest objects movable. To move a house, put it on wheels, or in this case, rollers. The rollers turn, pulling the house with them. Since the surface of the house is not pushing flat against the ground, friction is not holding it in place.

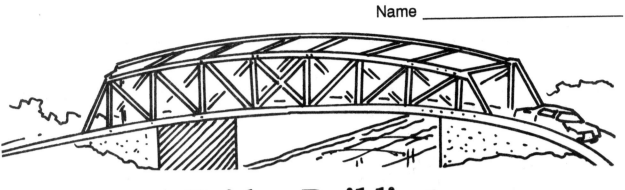

Bridge Building

Building a bridge is simple, isn't it? You just lay a board over a stream and there's a bridge. But what if the stream is a very wide river? What if it is a mile wide? What if a dozen army tanks need to cross that bridge? Do you have a board long enough and strong enough?

Engineers have developed ways to make buildings and bridges stronger. We can use steel and concrete and other materials which are strong and weather resistant. We can reinforce materials like wood and concrete with steel rods and beams to make those materials stronger. We can also use different shapes to strengthen the structure.

Materials: Several thick, heavy books, posterboard, scissors, masking tape, a protractor, and a ruler.

Procedure:
1. Cut a rectangular strip of posterboard 6 inches wide and 18 inches long. Make flat legs out of the posterboard to support this "bridge." Attach the legs with masking tape so the bridge stands up. Can your bridge support the weight of a book?_____

   Does it help if you add more legs?_____

2. Use pattern A on the next page to make new legs for your bridge. Remove the old legs and attach the new ones. Can your bridge support the weight of a book? _____

   Does it help if you add more legs?_____

   Does it matter where you put the legs? _____

3. Use pattern B on the next page to make more new legs for your bridge. Can your bridge support the weight of a book?_____

4. Use pattern C on the bottom of this page to make more new legs for your bridge. Can your new bridge support the weight of a book? _____

Evaluate:

1. Which kind of legs work best?

_____

2. Can any of the bridges support more than one book?

_____

3. Are some shapes stronger than others? _____

4. Does the shape of the bridge's supports affect the amount of weight the bridge can carry? _____

Use these patterns to cut legs for your bridge. Fold on the dotted lines and tape the open sides together. The final shape as seen from the top is drawn on the inside of each pattern piece.

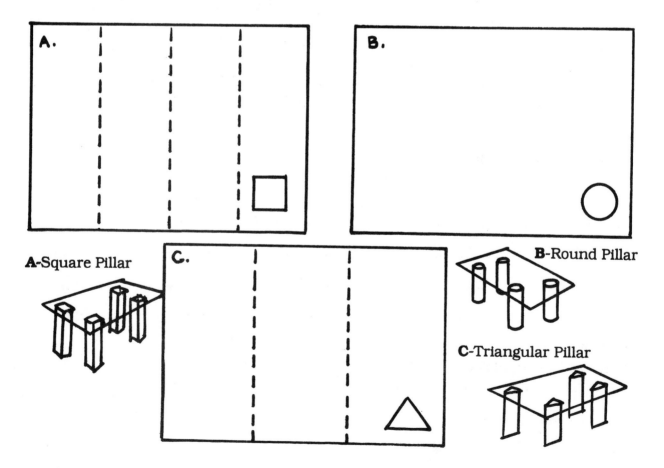

A.

B.

C.

A-Square Pillar

B-Round Pillar

C-Triangular Pillar

Suspension Bridges

In a suspension bridge, the weight of the bridge is hung or suspended from cables. The cables are made by twisting thin steel wires into strands. These strands are wrapped around plastic cores. It takes tremendous force to pull these cables apart, and they are used in some of the world's longest bridges. How does a suspension bridge work?

Materials: String, scissors, two straight-backed chairs, a ruler, and a weight from a scale or some other small weight.

Procedure:

1. Cut four pieces of string 20 inches long and six pieces of string 4 inches long.

2. Tie these pieces together as shown in the diagram below. You should have two separate lengths of string.

3. Place the two chairs back to back with a space between them. Tie the two lengths of string to the backs of the chairs as shown in the diagram to the right.

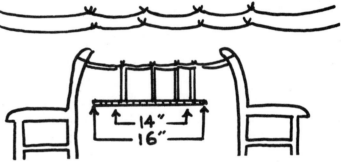

4. Cut two pieces of string (16 inches each) and two pieces of string (14 inches each). Tie them to the lengths of string which are attached to the chairs to form loops. Suspend the ruler from these loops.

5. Place the weight on the ruler. What happens?_____

_____

6. Move the weight to another spot on the ruler. Does the string change shape?

_____

7. Tilt the chair backs toward each other. What happens?

_____

Evaluate:

The cable of a suspension bridge works only when tension is applied to it, so it is called a *tensile structure*. If the tension is released, what happens to the bridge?

_____

Building Buildings

Builders do use columns and beams to build buildings, but they have designed one additional structure, the truss. A truss for a house is often triangle-shaped. Trusses can be combined to make other shapes. How does a truss work?

Materials: Popsicle sticks, white glue, and a stack of books.

Procedure:

1. Glue Popsicle sticks to make the shapes below. Make two sets of shapes a, b, and d and four sets of shape c. Set the shapes aside to dry.

2. When the shapes are thoroughly dry, test their strength. First support the two shapes from "a." above with two books as in the diagram to the side. Can you balance a book on top of these shapes without breaking them? How much of a load can they carry?

_____

In what direction do the pieces of the shape go when they break? _____

_____

3. Test the shapes from "b." above the same way. Use the diagram to the right to help you set up the shapes. Can they carry a heavier load?

_____

4. Test the shapes from "c." above. Arrange one pair of shapes like this:

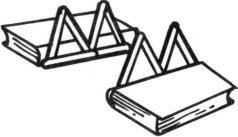

       FS-10169 Science and Technology: How Things Work

Arrange the second pair of shapes like this:

Which shape is stronger? _____

_____

5. In the space below, draw the movement of the pieces of the two pairs of shapes above when they collapse. Do they move the same way? _____

6. Test the shapes from "d." on the first page. Arrange the shapes as shown in the diagram to the right.

Can these shapes carry more of a load than the shapes in step 4? _____

Evaluate:
1. Does changing its shape make a structure stronger? _____

_____

2. What makes a truss strong? _____

_____

3. Of the shapes you tested, which ones would make good trusses for the roof of a house? _____

—— Shape and Strength ——

Can changing the shape of something make it stronger? A cardboard carton is strong because of the texture of the paper between the layers of flat paper. As a stunt, one company designed a paper bridge strong enough for a real car to cross over it! Another company has designed cardboard chairs strong enough to support a 200-pound person.

Materials: Three sheets of construction paper, cardboard from a heavy carton, scissors, marking pens, two pencils, string, a metal ruler, and several books.

Procedure:

1. Lay one sheet of paper between two towers of books. How much weight can it support?

_____

2. Fold the sheet of paper like an accordion and lay it between two towers of books as in the diagram to the right. How much weight can it support now?

_____

3. Bend a sheet of paper in a semicircle and support it with two towers of books as in the diagram to the right. How much weight can it support?_____

4. Use the marking pens to make lines on one sheet of paper according to the diagram on the next page. If you cannot make dotted lines, use two different marker colors. When you are finished, fold each separate line. Fold the solid lines down and the dotted lines up. Press against the ruler to help you fold.

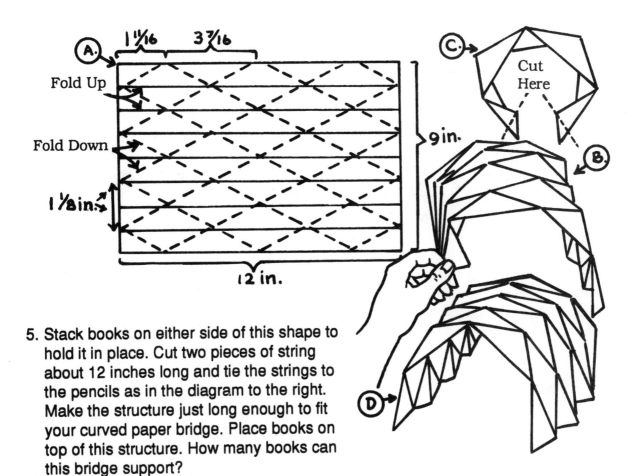

5. Stack books on either side of this shape to hold it in place. Cut two pieces of string about 12 inches long and tie the strings to the pencils as in the diagram to the right. Make the structure just long enough to fit your curved paper bridge. Place books on top of this structure. How many books can this bridge support?

_____

Evaluate:

1. Are some shapes stronger than others? _____

_____

2. Which of the shapes you made would be best for bridges and roofs of buildings? Why?

_____

_____

3. Examine the cardboard in a heavy carton. What is the shape that makes this stronger than flat posterboard or gift box cardboard? Draw the shape in the space below.

Name _____

A Pump

A water pump pulls water up out of the ground. A bicycle pump pushes air into the tires. How do these pumps work?

Materials: A paper towel tube, a soda straw, a plastic container lid, posterboard, masking tape, scissors, and a sheet of paper.

Procedure:

1. Cut a ½" square out of opposite sides of one end of the tube. Cut a circle out of the posterboard that will just fit over one end of the paper towel tube. Cut a circle out of the container lid that will just fit inside the paper towel tube. This circle must be able to move freely, but not have much air space around its perimeter.

2. Tape the straw to the plastic disc.

3. Cut two ¾" squares of paper. Place tape on one side of one square and tape it to the outside of the tube over one of the ½" square openings. It must be possible for it to flap like a door.

4. Tape the second square to the inside of the opposite ½" opening. Again it must be possible for it to flap like a door, but the door must open inward to the inside of the tube. (See the diagram to the right.)

5. Cover the bottom of the tube (the end with the doors) with the posterboard disc. Tape the disc on the tube so there are no airholes around the edges of the disc.

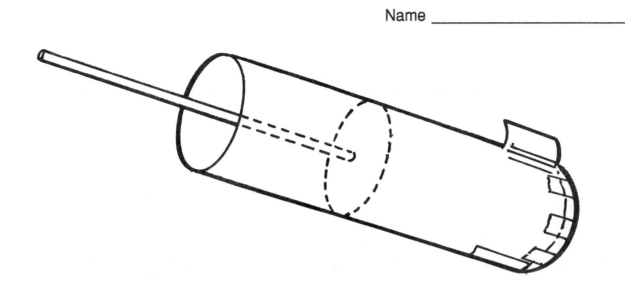

6. Insert the plastic disc in the other end of the tube with the straw sticking up for a handle. Use the straw to push the disc down the tube. Watch the paper doors carefully while you do this. What happens? _____

_____

7. Pull the straw and the plastic disc back up the tube. Watch the paper doors carefully. What happens? _____

_____

Evaluate:

1. The paper door which flaps inward is the air or water intake valve of a pump. The paper door which flaps outward is the air or water output valve of a pump. Which valve pumps air into the tire of a bicycle? _____

2. Which valve pulls water up from the well? _____

3. On the diagram of a pump below, place arrows to show the direction that the water or air flows.

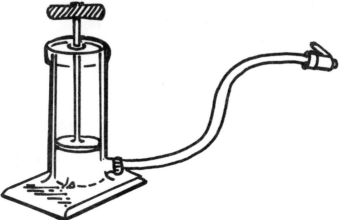

Levers

We use levers everyday. Pianos, manual typewriters, nail clippers, bathroom scales, and all types of weighing machines, parking meters, vending machines, and car jacks use levers. A lever is simply a bar which rests on a pivot point, called the fulcrum, to lift a load. There are three different types of levers—first-, second-, and third-class levers.

First-Class Levers:

The seesaw or teeter-totter is a good example of a first-class lever. The load sits on one end, the fulcrum is under the middle of the lever, and the effort is at the other end of the lever.

Materials: Two rulers, play dough or modeling clay, posterboard, scissors, and masking tape.

Procedure:

1. Trace the pattern at the bottom of page 60 onto a piece of posterboard and cut it out. Fold along the dotted lines and tape the open side to form a pyramid shape. This is the fulcrum.

2. Make small balls of equal size and weight out of the play dough or clay. Set up the ruler (lever) and fulcrum on a table as shown in the diagram to the right. Place a ball of play dough on each end and move the ruler until it balances. At what point on the ruler does it balance?_____

_____

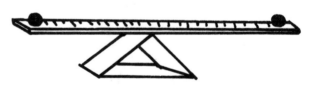

3. Place two balls of play dough on one end and one ball of dough on the other end. At what point does it balance?

_____

4. Push the end of the ruler with two balls all the way down to the table and measure the height of the ball on the other end. How high is it off the table? _____

_____

5. Push the end of the ruler with one ball all the way down to the table and measure the height of the ball on the other end. How high is it off the table?

Evaluate:

1. Look at your answers to questions #2 and #3. What happens when the weight on the load end is twice as heavy as the weight on the effort end of the lever? What is the difference in the length of the lever? _____

   _____

2. Look at your answers to questions #4 and #5. What happens to the height of the lever when the load is twice as heavy as the effort? _____

   _____

Second-Class Levers:

A wheelbarrow is a good example of a second-class lever. For this kind of lever, the fulcrum is at one end, the effort is at the other end and the load is in the middle. A nutcracker is another example of this kind of lever.

Materials: Round toothpicks.

Procedure:

1. Place one toothpick over your middle finger and under your index and ring fingers on one hand. Place it close to the tips of your fingers (See the diagram to the right.) Press down on the toothpick and try to break it. What happens? Can you break it? _____

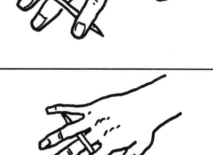

2. Place the toothpick close to the palm of your hand but still over your middle finger and under your index and ring fingers. (See the diagram to the right.) Can you break the toothpick now?_____

Evaluate:

1. Look at the illustration above. The fulcrum in the experiment above is the point where your fingers join your hand. Your index and ring fingers are the effort. Is it easier to break the toothpick (does it require less force) when the toothpick is near the fulcrum or farther away?_____

2. Look at the picture of the nutcracker to the right. Draw a nut in the spot where it would be easiest to crack it open.

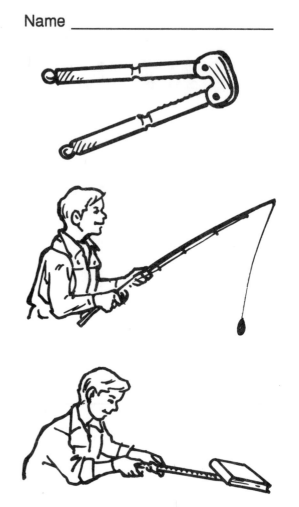

Third-Class Lever:

A fishing rod is a good example of a third-class lever. The fulcrum is on one end, the load is on the other end and the effort is in the middle. Look at the picture to the right.

Materials: A yardstick and a paperback book.

Procedure:

1. Place the paperback book on one end of the yardstick. Place one hand under the opposite end of the yardstick. This hand is just to hold the yardstick steady. It is the fulcrum. Do not do any lifting with this hand. Place your other hand two inches from the first hand and try to lift the book on the other end. What happens? Is it easy?

_____

_____

_____

2. Place the lifting hand 18 inches from the fulcrum hand (nearer to the book). Lift the book again. Is it easier this time?

_____

Evaluate:

A third-class lever is easier to use when the force is (nearer to/farther from) the load. (circle one)

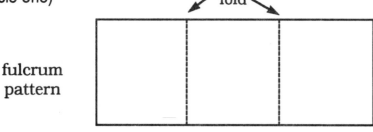

fulcrum pattern

Brakes

Brakes work because of friction. When you push something, you feel a force pushing back, a resistance. This resistance is *friction*.

Bobsled Brakes

A bobsled travels down icy slopes at speeds in excess of 70 miles per hour. How do you stop a fast-moving bobsled on an icy stretch? One rider pulls a lever which depresses the brake. The brake is a piece of metal. Circle the picture below that shows a bobsled brake. Why did you make that choice?

1. _____
   _____
   _____
   _____

2. Can you think of other types of brakes that are similar to the bobsled's brakes?

Automobile Disc Brakes

The wheels of cars with disc brakes have a disc, a circle of metal attached to the wheel. The disc rotates with the wheel and two small pads attached to calipers (devices that squeeze the pads toward each other) press against the disc.

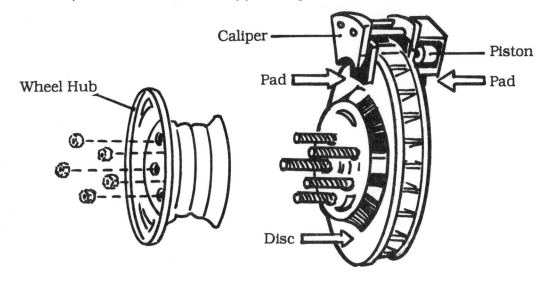

Materials: A pair of tweezers, string, scissors, and plastic top from margarine or whipped topping container.

Procedure:

1. Cut a piece of string 12 inches long. Pierce the center of the plastic top and thread the string through the hole. (See the diagram to the right.)

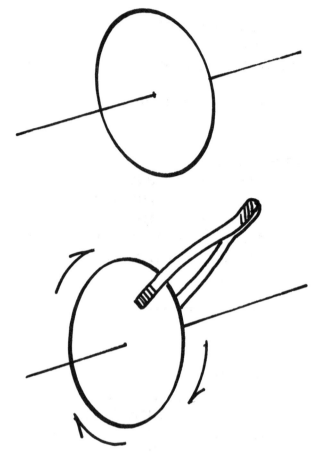

2. Have another person hold the ends of the string taut. Hold the tweezers near the edge of the top with the top between the open pincers of the tweezers.

3. Spin the top rapidly. Close the pincers of the tweezers. What happens? _____

    _____

    _____

Disc brakes are much better than conventional brakes in wet weather because the friction of the pads on the disc makes them very hot. This dries any moisture that is on the smooth surfaces of the brakes. Why is this such an advantage? (HINT: Think of what happens when you walk on a wet floor with smooth, slippery shoes.)

Moving Heavy Things

How can you reduce friction? You can grease or oil a surface or make it smoother. Suppose you want to move something very heavy like a house. You cannot just tie a rope around it and drag it. What can you do?

Materials: Four pieces of ¼" dowel cut 12" in length, three heavy books, and heavy string.

Procedure:

1. Pile the books in a stack on a table and tie the string around the stack as in the diagram to the right. Using one finger, pull the string. Is it easy to move the stack of books?

_____

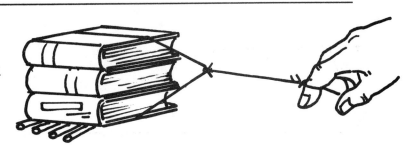

2. Place the dowels under the stack of books as in the diagram to the right. Using the same finger, pull the string. Is it easy to move the stack of books this time?

_____

3. Was it easier to pull the stack of books when they were on the dowel rollers or when they were flat on the table? _____

Evaluate:

1. When the books were lying flat on the table, how much of the bottom cover of the bottom book was touching the table?

_____

2. When the books were lying on top of the dowel rollers, how much of the bottom cover of the bottom book was touching the table?_____

3. When less of the book's surface was touching the table it was (easier/harder) to move.

4. What is one way you can reduce friction? _____

_____

Chapter Five

Locomotion

─── Teacher Notes ───

This chapter explains the principles behind many of our vehicles and modes of transportation. The topics include bicycle gears, water skis, sailboats, motorboat propellers, submarines, hot air balloons, gliders, airplanes, and helicopters.

Bicycle Gears

This activity demonstrates the principles behind gears. If you have someone who can crochet, a very loose crochet chain is the fastest way to make this bicycle chain. The directions demonstrate the ten-finger method of creating a crochet chain. Following this experiment, allow students to expand their knowledge of gears by creating gears that mesh with other gears. Invite them to create a toy or device of their own design that uses gears. Have students demonstrate and display their creations. Make a bulletin board display showing machines that use gears to accompany this activity. Include clocks, cars and other vehicles, cranes, windmills, ships, and simple devices such as can openers.

Water Skis

Water skis will float by themselves, but they are too small to support the weight of a person. That is why you cannot walk on water by yourself when you are wearing water skis. Heavier people require a faster-moving boat because they require more lift. The more force you have pushing down (weight) the more force you need pulling up to lift that weight out of the water.

This simple experiment demonstrates the principle of hydrodynamic lift. The needle is an exaggerated ski shape. Point out that the eye end of the needle is rounded just like the tip of a water ski. This makes the ski (or needle in this case) move more smoothly through the water. The tip of a ski is also bent upward slightly.

Sailboats and Sailboat Sails

Make a bulletin board display of different sailing craft to accompany this activity. If you cannot find pictures of Chinese junks, Phoenician sailboats, clipper ships, and yachts, ask artistic students to draw them. Have students research different types of sailboats and write a short report to accompany the illustrations.

Sheets of balsa wood can be obtained at craft stores. This is a fairly fragile wood, so caution students to be careful and gentle when cutting and handling their crafts. Expand this activity by allowing students to experiment with different hull and sail designs. Which designs produce the fastest sailboats? The slowest?

Motorboats

This balsa boat is self-propelled. The electrical tape has very good adhesive qualities and is waterproof, so do not substitute another kind of tape. Motorboat propellers usually double as the rudder as well. To turn the boat, you turn the whole propeller assembly. Since this propeller assembly is not movable, this design includes a rudder.

Submarines

How can a heavy ship float when a tiny penny sinks? This activity demonstrates the concepts of density and buoyancy. An object which is less dense than water will float. Buoyancy is dependent on the density of an object in relation to the density of water. (This is why an egg will float in heavily salted water. The salt water is more dense than the egg. The egg will not float in unsalted water.) As you spread the weight of an object out over a greater surface area, its density relative to any one spot in the water is less. The load is shared with all of the surface of the water that the object is touching. Compare this to a heavy log with five people to carry it. If you stand the log on end so that the entire load rests on one person, it is very heavy and the one person cannot carry it. If you turn the log on one side so that five people are carrying it, the load is lighter for that one person and all five people can carry it.

Hot Air Balloons

Hot air balloons use the principle that hot air is less dense than cold air. Remind students that when you warm gases, they expand and the molecules move farther away from each other. This means that you have fewer molecules of the gas in any given area and fewer molecules weigh less. The envelope of this balloon is fragile, so caution students to be gentle with it.

Gliders

Gliders work because of their wide wingspan. Jet planes do not glide well. Some small airplanes do glide well, which is a great advantage if the engine cuts out. Since a glider has no engine, it is at the mercy of the air currents. What happens when a glider hits a hot air current? (It rises.) What happens when a glider hits a cold air current? (It falls.) Hang gliders work on these same principles.

Airplanes

Make a bulletin board to accompany this activity by collecting pictures and drawings of different airplane designs from the early Wright brothers design to the jets and space shuttle of today. Discuss the designs, comparing and contrasting wing designs, body shapes, engines, and capabilities of the different aircraft. Have students research and write short reports on the designs of their choice and the men who built and flew them. Include the mythical Icarus, the Wright brothers, the astronauts, Leonardo da Vinci's designs, Louis Blériot of France, Amelia Earhart, the Sopwith Camel, Fokker Triplanes, the Boeing 314 Clipper, the Messerschmitt Bf 109, Amy Johnson (made history in 1930 by flying from England to Australia), Chuck Yeager (in 1947, he broke the "sound barrier" in a Bell X-1), and the *Concorde*.

Helicopters

Helicopters have the great capacity to take off and land vertically. This activity demonstrates the lift effect of the rotor blades. The "Boomerangs" activity which follows is an extension of and companion to this experiment.

Boomerangs

If helicopters did not have movable blades on the rotors, they would "boomerang." The force of the lift increases as the blade moves forward, and if the helicopter blades were stationary this would create a very unstable situation. Instead, the blades flap up and down with the variations in lift and the pilot steers the helicopter by tilting the blades.

Bicycle Gears

A **gear** is a circle or disc which rotates on a shaft. On a bicycle with one gear there is just one disc. On a bicycle with several gears there are several discs side-by-side. A bicycle uses a **chain drive** where the pedals are attached to one gear and a chain connects this disc to another disc on the rear wheel. On a chain drive, the discs are called **sprockets.** A bicycle with several gears has a sprocket for every gear on the rear wheel. When you change gears, the chain slips to a different sprocket. The larger sprockets are for the higher gears; the smaller sprockets are for lower gears.

Materials: Yarn, posterboard, scissors, two soda straws, marking pens, two identical straight-backed chairs, and masking tape.

Procedure:

1. Make a loose chain out of the yarn using the diagram below to show you how. The chain should be 24" long. Make certain you can insert your finger into each link of the chain.

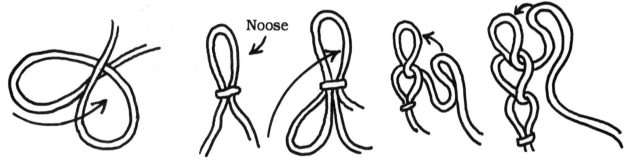

Noose

2. Cut out the patterns on the second page of this activity and trace each pattern onto posterboard. Cut out each posterboard piece carefully. You need each of the teeth in each gear! In the center of each gear, cut a hole that will exactly fit around a soda straw. (A one-hole punch makes a perfect-sized hole.)

3. Draw a design on the wheel shape. This will make the speed of the wheel easier to determine.

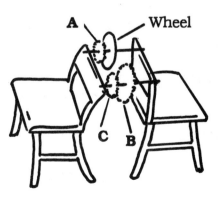

A   Wheel

C   B

4. Mount the gears and the wheel as shown in the diagram to the right. Leave a ½" space between the gears. Notice that gear A goes on its own straw. The other two go together on another straw. Tape all of the discs in place so they cannot move off their straw.

5. Put the chairs six inches apart with their backs parallel to each other. Mount the two straws on the backs of the chairs as shown at the right. Link the yarn chain around the two sets of gears, using the smallest sprocket on the straw with two gears. Tie the yarn chain together at the ends and snip off the extra yarn.

6. Turn the single disc. What happens to your "wheel"?

_____

7. Move the yarn chain to the larger sprocket. Turn the single disc. What happens to your "wheel"? _____

_____

Evaluate:

In the sentences below, circle the correct answer.

1. In a chain drive, the smaller sprocket makes the wheel move more (quickly/slowly).

2. The larger sprocket makes the wheel move more (quickly/slowly).

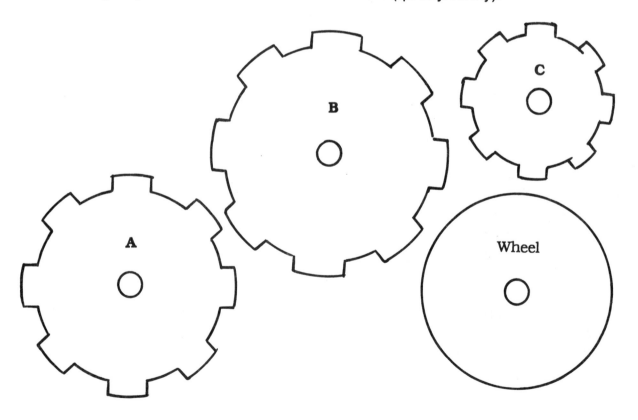

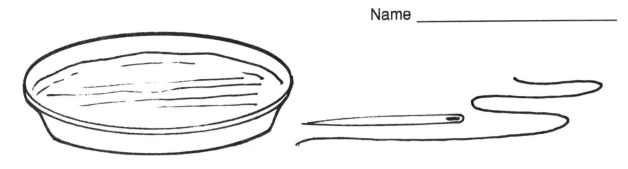

Water Skis

When you are on water skis and a motorboat is pulling you, you can ride the surface of the water. Why can't you walk on the surface of the water by yourself when you are wearing the skis? Why does the boat have to move more rapidly to pull heavier people?

The principle behind the water ski is **hydrodynamic lift.** The skis have to be at an angle to the water's surface, and the force of the boat moving forward pulls them parallel to the surface. The force of the water pushes upward on the skis while the boat pulls them forward. The more rapidly the boat moves, the greater the lift.

Materials: A needle, two feet of thread, and a large baking pan full of water.

Procedure:

1. Thread the needle. Pull the thread so the two sides are even. Wind the loose ends around your finger so the length of the thread between your finger and the needle is six inches. (See the diagram to the right.)

2. Drop the needle in the water. What happens?_____

_____

3. Angle the needle so the eye is near the surface of the water and the tip is pointing toward the bottom of the pan. (See the diagram to the right.) Pull the needle in circles around the pan. Pull it in slow circles at first. What happens? _____

4. Pull the needle in fast circles, being careful not to pull the needle out of the water. What happens? _____

_____

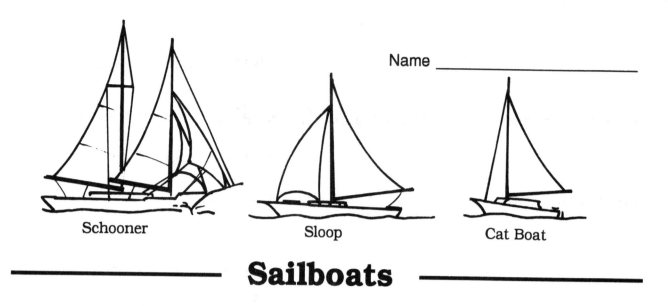

Schooner   Sloop   Cat Boat

Name _____

Sailboats

Sailboats were first invented and used between 4,000 and 6,000 years ago. The ancient Egyptians were using sailboats by 2000 B.C. The clipper ships of the 1800s were the largest and fastest of the sailing ships. These immense ships had from three to six masts with up to 35 square sails and crews of up to 60 people to man these sails. These fast sailing ships could carry a large cargo and cross the Atlantic Ocean in less than two weeks.

Most modern sailboats use two triangular sails. The **foresail** or **jib** is the front sail. The **mainsail** is larger and is positioned behind the mast. The mainsail is attached at the bottom to a movable **boom.** The boom is used to swing the sail around so that it faces the wind.

If the wind is not blowing in the right direction, the sailor **tacks** the sail or sets it at an angle to the wind. The boat is pointed in the opposite direction and follows a zigzag course to get to its destination. The **rudder** on the bottom or **hull** of the boat is used to steer the boat. The **keel,** a fin-shaped piece on the underside of the hull, acts as a weight to keep the boat upright and a counter balance to the sail and the wind. Without the keel, the boat would skid and slide around in the water. Label these parts on the sailboat below.

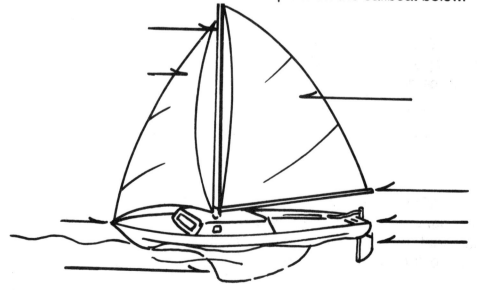

Sailboat Sails

How do the sails of a sailboat work?

Materials: A sheet of balsa wood or cork, round toothpicks, a 9" x 13" baking pan filled with water to a depth of 1", scissors, and paper.

Procedure:

1. Use the pattern on the next page to cut a hull out of the balsa wood or cork.

2. Cut out the sail and stick a toothpick through it at the black dots. (See the diagram at the right.)

3. Insert the toothpick in the center of the balsa wood or cork. Stick it just enough to hold it steady. Do not make a large hole. (See the diagram to the right.)

4. Turn the paper sail so it is parallel to the boat hull and set the boat in the water. Blow straight at the boat from behind. What happens?_____

_____

5. Turn the paper sail so it is at right angles to the boat hull. In sailing terms this is called *running*. Blow straight at the boat from behind. What happens? _____

_____

6. Turn the paper sail at the angle shown in the diagram to the right. This is called *reaching* in sailing terms. What happens when you blow on the boat from the direction indicated by the arrow? _____

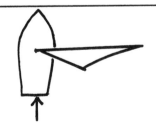

Below are the different sail positions used by sailors. Set your sails according to each position and blow at the boat according to the direction indicated by the arrow. Record your observations for each position in the blanks below. You have already done "running" and "reaching" so there is not a space for those two positions.

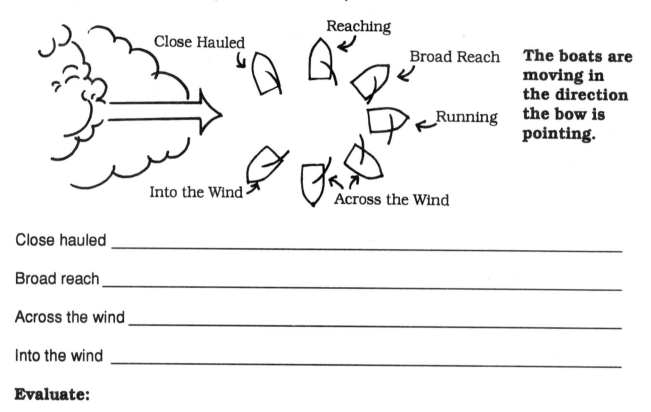

Close hauled _____

Broad reach _____

Across the wind _____

Into the wind _____

Evaluate:

Which position makes the boat move most rapidly? _____

_____

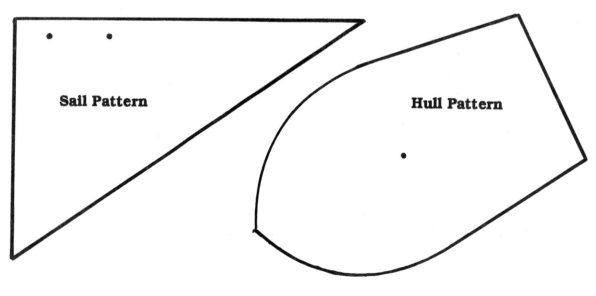

Motorboats

Motorboats are driven by propellers. As the blades of the propeller move, they push the water in front of the blades to the back of the boat. The force of this thrust pushes the boat forward. In addition, the movement of the water creates a lower water pressure in front of the propeller. This in turn creates a suction force which pulls the propeller forward and the boat with it. The combination of thrust and suction propels the boat through the water.

Materials: A plastic container lid, scissors, electrical tape, a ⅛" thick rubber band, a sheet of cork or balsa wood, a soda straw, a crochet hook, a baking pan half full of water, a small hex nut, and a small nail.

Procedure:

1. Use the pattern on the next page to cut out a hull for your boat. Use the cork or balsa wood for the hull. Cut the soda straw exactly the same length as your hull and tape it to the underside of the hull. Slide the straw so it extends ¼" beyond the back of the hull. (See the diagram to the right.)

2. Use the pattern on the next page to cut a propeller shape out of the plastic container lid. Bend the blades on the dotted lines. (See the diagram to the right.)

3. Loop the rubber band around the nail and thread it through the soda straw from the front (bow) of the boat to the back (stern). Use the crochet hook to pull the rubber band through the soda straw. Thread the rubber band through the hex nut and then loop this end around the prong on the propeller blade. (See the diagram to the right.)

4. Tape the nail on the top (deck) of the boat so it cannot move. (See the diagram to the right.)

5. Turn the propeller several times to wind it up. Hold the propeller to keep it from unwinding. Set the boat in the water and let it go. What happens?

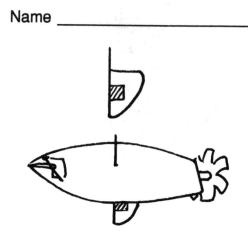

6. Use the rudder pattern to cut a rudder out of cork or balsa wood. Fasten it to a toothpick with electrical tape. See the diagram at the right for help.

7. Stick the end of the toothpick up through the center of the boat. Use this end of the toothpick as a handle to turn the rudder. (See the diagram at right.)

8. Set the rudder straight ahead and wind the propeller. Which way does the boat move? _____

9. Turn the rudder to the right and wind the propeller. Which way does the boat move?

_____

10. Turn the rudder to the left and wind the propeller. Which way does the boat move?

_____

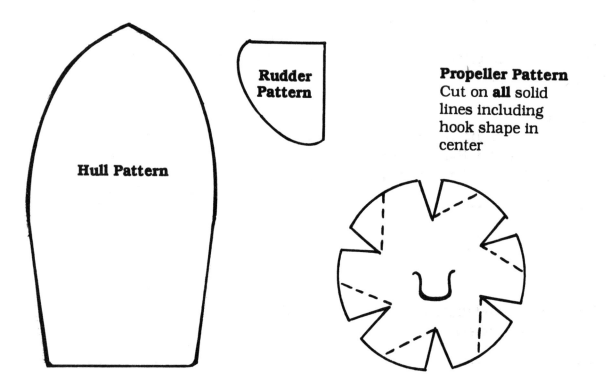

Hull Pattern

Rudder Pattern

Propeller Pattern
Cut on **all** solid lines including hook shape in center

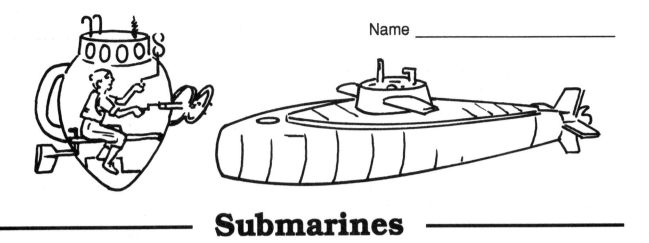

Submarines

In 1776, an American named David Bushnell invented a one-man submarine named the Turtle. The Turtle had hand-cranked propellers and a drill on the top. The Turtle was supposed to move under the hull of a British warship and then drill a hole in the bottom of the warship. A charge of gunpowder would be placed in the hole and ignited to blow up the warship. Unfortunately, the British warships had copper-covered hulls which were too strong for the drills.

Modern submarines have propellers to push them through the water and a much more complex design than the Turtle. The hull has a double wall for ballast to allow it to submerge and then float back up to the top. Water is run into the wall when the submarine is to go down under the water and then pumped out and replaced with compressed air when the submarine needs to go back up to the surface. How does this work?

Materials: A small glass jar with a water-tight lid, modeling clay, a penny, and a bowl with enough water to completely submerge the jar.

Procedure:

1. Fill the jar to the top and cap it. Make certain there is no air in it. Place the water-filled jar in the bowl of water. What happens?_____

   _____

2. Empty the jar and recap it. Place it in the bowl of water. What happens?_____

   _____

3. Push the air-filled jar under the surface of the water and let go. What happens? _____

4. Drop the penny in the water. What happens? _____
_____

5. Make a ball of the clay and place it in the water. What happens? _____
_____

6. Take the clay out of the water and mold it into a boat shape. Place it back into the water. What happens? _____

Evaluate:

1. Which weighs more, the empty jar or the penny? _____

2. Which covers a larger surface area, the jar or the penny? _____

3. The weight of the empty jar is spread out over a much larger area than that of the penny. This means that in any one spot it is not as heavy as the water. It is less **dense** than the water. This causes it to float in the water. We say the jar is **buoyant.** Why does the water-filled jar sink? _____
_____

4. Will the jar sink if it is just partly filled with water? (Try it and see.) _____
_____

5. Why does the ball of clay sink? _____
_____

6. Why does the boat made of clay float? _____
_____

Hot Air Balloons

When air molecules are warmed, they move farther apart, making the hot air less dense than the cold air. This makes the hot air rise. What happens when you heat the air inside a balloon?

Materials: Tissue paper, thread, several pennies, tape, scissors, glue, and a hair dryer.

Procedure:

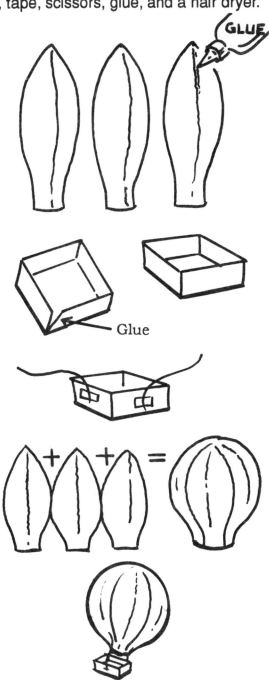

1. Use the pattern on page 79 to cut six tissue paper pieces for the **envelope** of the balloon. Make a line of glue along one edge of three of these patterns. Attach one unglued pattern piece to each of these glued pieces to make three pairs as shown in the diagram to the right. Set these pairs aside to dry.

2. Cut out the basket shape on page 79 and fold it on the dotted lines. Place glue on the tabs that say "glue" and fasten the sides of the basket together. (See the diagram at the right.)

3. Cut four pieces of thread. Each one should be 6" long. Attach the threads to the four corners of the basket with a small amount of tape. (See the diagram at the right.)

4. Place glue on one edge of each pair of envelope pieces and glue the pairs together to make a complete balloon shape. Set the envelope aside to dry. (See the diagram at the right.)

5. When the envelope is completely dry, attach the four strings of the basket to it with small amounts of tape. (See the diagram at the right.)

6. A gas burner heats the air inside a hot air balloon. A gas burner would be dangerous with this paper balloon, so a hair dryer is your substitute. Push the basket of your balloon to the side, being careful not to tear it loose from the balloon. Fit the open part of your envelope over the nozzle of the hair dryer and turn the dryer on medium. When the balloon is inflated, let it go. What happens? _____

7. Put a penny in the basket of your balloon and repeat step six. What happens?

_____

8. How many pennies can your balloon hold and still fly?

_____

Evaluate:

1. Hot air balloons rise because hot air is (lighter/heavier) than cold air. (circle one)

2. A hot air balloon can rise with some weight in its basket. Is there a limit to the amount of weight a hot air balloon can carry? _____

3. What happens if the load in the basket of the balloon is too heavy? _____

_____

4. If you were in a hot air balloon and it was not rising high enough, what could you do to make it rise higher? _____

_____

Balloon Patterns

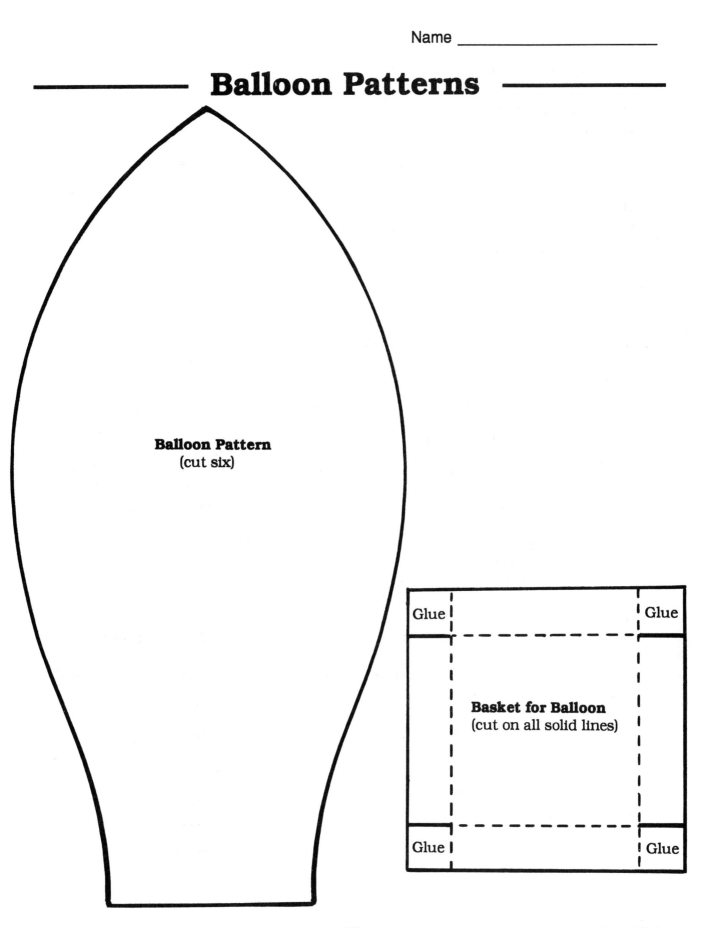

Balloon Pattern
(cut six)

Basket for Balloon
(cut on all solid lines)

Glue

Glue

Glue

Glue

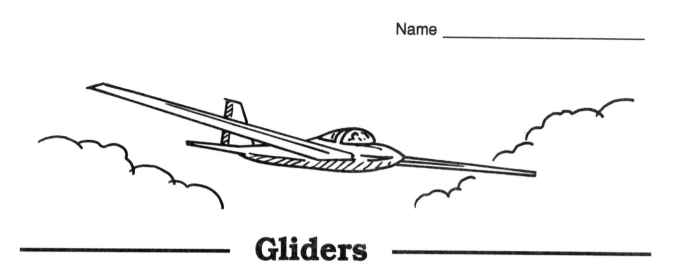

Gliders

A glider looks like an airplane but it has no engine. To get airborne, an airplane tows it up into the air. When it is airborne, the towline is released and the glider glides through the sky and back to the earth. The glider has long, straight wings to keep it aloft. When air moves quickly, its pressure drops. The air on top of a glider or airplane wing moves quickly. This means the air pressure under the wing is greater than the air pressure on top of the wing and the wing is pushed upward.

Materials: Three sheets of paper.

Procedure:

1. Hold the paper by the corners on one side so it flops down in front of you. See the diagram to the right for help.

2. Blow hard across the top of the paper.
   What happens? Does the paper go up or down? _____

3. Use two pieces of paper to fold paper airplanes according to the diagrams on the next page. Fly them both. Which flies farthest? _____

   Which stays airborne longest? _____

4. Use the third sheet of paper to design your own paper airplane. Does yours fly longer or farther than the other designs? _____

Evaluate:
Why do you think one plane flies farther and stays airborne longer than the other? What is the difference between the two? _____

_____

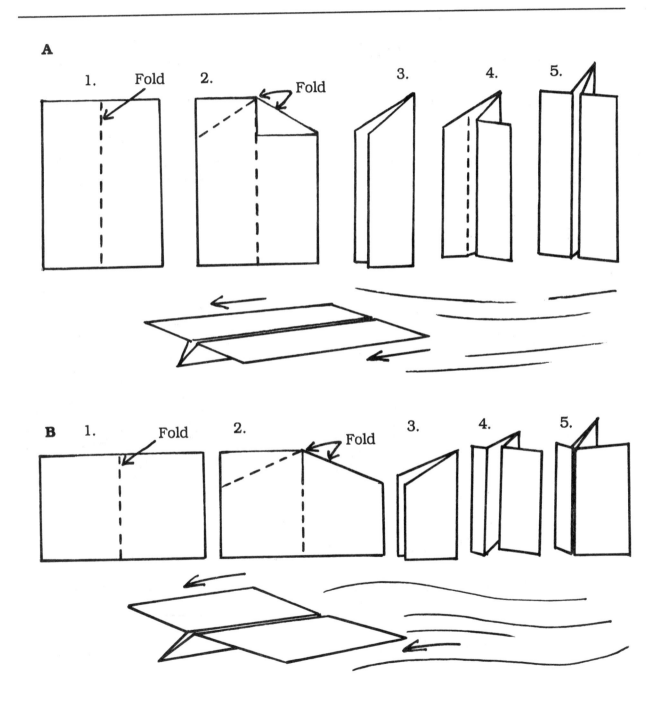

Airplanes

The wings of airplanes are designed to increase the speed of the air as it flows over the wing. The wings have flaps called **ailerons** that can be moved up and down to increase the area of the wing and increase the speed of the air over the top of the wing or to increase the drag or resistance of the plane and slow it down. These flaps also help to steer the plane. A rudder on the tail of the plane also swivels to help the plane turn.

Materials: A piece of paper, a stapler, and scissors.

Procedure:

1. Fold the paper according to the diagram below. Staple the airplane at the top to hold it together.

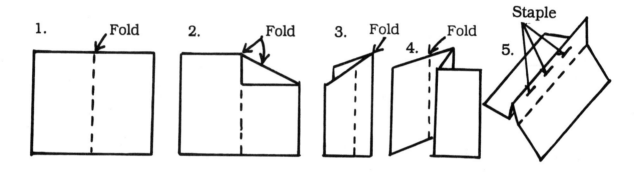

2. Fly your airplane and note how it flies. Does it turn or curve or roll over? _____
   Cut ailerons in each wing according to the diagram below.

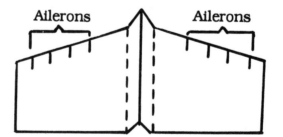

3. Fold the ailerons up on one wing and down on the other wing. Fly your airplane again. What difference does this make? _____

4. Experiment with folding the ailerons different ways. Note which way you folded the ailerons and how the plane flies. Record your observations on the back of this sheet.

Name _____

Helicopters

Helicopters can rise straight up in the air and can hover. They could not do this if they had fixed wings like airplanes. The rotor blades on top spin and pull the helicopter off the ground.

Materials: A hammer, a small block of wood, a nail, an empty thread spool, scissors, string, glue, and a plastic container lid.

Procedure:

1. Use the pattern at the bottom of the page to cut out model rotor blades. Glue this blade to the top of the empty spool of thread and set it aside to dry. (See the diagram at the right.)

2. Hammer the nail through the board. Turn the board so the nail sticks straight up in the air. Place the spool on the nail.

3. Wind one yard of string around the spool. Pull the loose end quickly so the spool spins very rapidly. What happens? _____

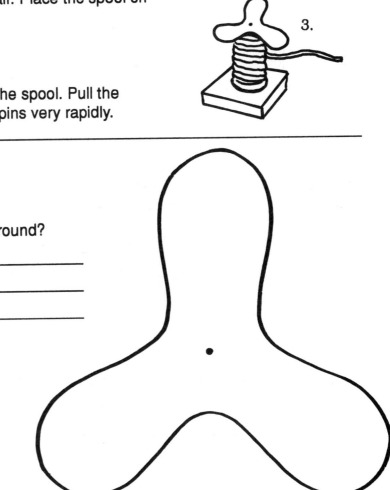

Evaluate:
How does a helicopter get off the ground?

_____

_____

_____

Boomerangs

Helicopters have hinged blades on their rotors. If the blades were not hinged, they would boomerang. How does a boomerang work?

Materials: Posterboard and scissors.

Procedure: Use the patterns below to cut out two boomerang shapes. Gently toss them in the air. What is the pattern of their flight? _____

Evaluate:
What would happen to a helicopter if the blades were stationary? _____
_____

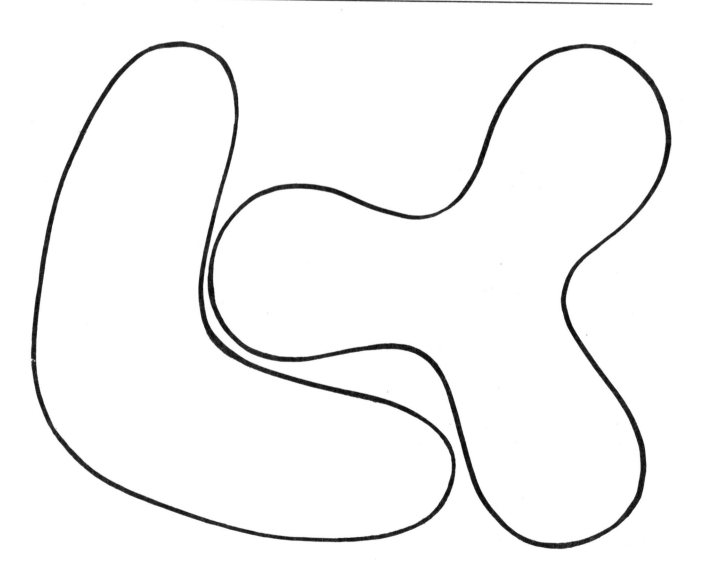

Chapter Six

Communication

————— Teacher Notes —————

Papermaking, printing, the telephone, radio, radar, television, calculators, computers, and binary code are the topics covered in this chapter. Make a bulletin board display to accompany this chapter that includes pictures of the different means of communication. Expand the chapter by including speech, sign language, telegraphs and Morse code, semaphore signals, Braille, and the arts on your bulletin board. Discuss these methods of communication. How can a computer help a person who cannot speak to communicate? How can a blind person read? How can a deaf person communicate? (Through sign language, through printing and writing, through the arts, through a computer...) We all have many different means of communicating.

Making Paper

Originally, cotton and linen fibers were the basic raw material for paper. Wood pulp is more commonly used today, although some fine papers still use cotton and linen fibers (particularly high grade art papers). Recycled paper is made largely from newspapers, magazines, and other printed papers. In ancient Egypt, paper was made from the papyrus plant, and it is from this plant and this Egyptian paper that we get the name paper. The Egyptians cut the papyrus in thin strips and crisscrossed the strips to form a woven paper layer which they pressed into sheets. Paper using wood fibers was invented in A.D.105 by a Chinese man named Ts'ai Lun. He made his paper out of the inner bark of the mulberry tree. Many different kinds of wood are used today.

In this activity, students use recycled newspaper pulp to make a new sheet of paper. This paper will be somewhat dark in color because the newspaper dye is not removed. If you have access to the ends of newsprint rolls (ask your local newspaper printing office) you may make a light, pastel paper or brighter colored paper. Paper towels also make a good pulp.

Students can help make their own screens to drain the water out of the pulp. Make a frame from thin wood strips or purchase pre-cut canvas stretchers from an art supply store. Staple nylon net or window screen to the frame. Pull the mesh taut and staple it to the sides of the frame for added strength. The size suggested on the activity sheet is 9" x 12" to accommodate the length of the rolling pin.

Printing

As the student sheet points out, Gutenberg was not the first to invent movable type. His printing press, however, was a first and paved the way for making books accessible to the general population. Discuss the importance of Gutenberg's invention and its impact on our lives today. How did the printing press influence the formation of our country in colonial days? What was Gutenberg's invention first used for?

The process of printing involves impressing an inked image onto a sheet of paper. The linoleum block print, which is the first part of the student activity, leaves a mirror image on the paper. Compare this to the offset printing press which makes a mirror image on the blanket cylinder. (The blanket cylinder is like the linoleum block.)

The four-color printing process used to print many color pictures is the focus of the last part of the student activity. For a follow-up activity, give students small quantities of paint in each of the four colors, a paintbrush, and a large sheet of construction paper. Invite them to make small patches of as many different colors as possible using only red, blue, yellow, and black. Point out that using different proportions of the colors will yield different results. For instance, two drops of yellow plus one drop of red gives a color different from two drops of red plus one drop of yellow. Instruct them to keep the patches of paint small, no larger than an inch in diameter.

The Telephone

Alexander Graham Bell invented the telephone in 1876, using an iron disc as the diaphragm. He was upstairs and telephoned his assistant, Mr. Watson, downstairs giving us this historic first phone message: "Mr. Watson, come here, I want you." Modern telephones are much more complex. The diaphragm is adjacent to carbon granules which vary the current flow through the microphone. The vibrations are converted to digital signals and "multiplexed" so that one individual phone line can carry several different phone conversations.

The student experiment demonstrates a modified version of Alexander Graham Bell's first design. The diaphragms are paper and the cones are Styrofoam cups. Students may have to speak very loudly into this telephone in order to be heard.

Radio

A simple radio receiver is not all that complex or difficult to build, but the components are not everyday household items. If you have students who are interested, invite them to research the subject and build one with the help of a parent or other adult. This activity sheet gives a basic explanation of the radio and radio frequencies.

Radar

Radar was initially developed as a means of defense during World War II, but the peacetime applications have been even greater. Radar is the chief means of tracking airplanes and directing air traffic at airports. Arrange a field trip to an airport if possible and have students see firsthand the advantages and uses of radar. Radar is also used for tracking ships and navigating ships.

Television

This experiment demonstrates the way the television camera and picture tubes produce what we perceive as moving colored pictures on the screen of a television. The first part of the activity demonstrates the blending of small spots of color to create the image of a totally different color. Show students pictures by the artist Georges Seurat, who developed *pointillism*. Seurat uses small dots of different colors to create shades and shapes. (You can find copies of his works such as *Side Show* and *Bather*s in art texts such as Janson's *History of Art*. The picture *Side Show* is housed in The Metropolitan Museum of Art.) How does the television screen adapt the artist's process?

The second part of this activity is a simple demonstration of the way the brain translates as movement a series of rapidly changing images. The trick is to flip the pages quickly while allowing the eye to see enough of the picture to hold the image.

Calculators, Computers, and Binary Code

Binary code is the basis of calculators and computers, as this activity explains. The binary code is not difficult if the student can think in terms of one-zero, not ten and one-one, not eleven. The picture on the second page of this activity provides additional practice.

Making Paper

Trees are the main ingredient in papermaking. The trees are cut, stripped of their bark, and chopped into chips. The chips are treated with chemicals or ground to make a pulp. The pulp may be mixed with cotton rags to add strength to the paper. The pulp is mixed with more chemicals, such as sizing which waterproofs the paper and dyes which give it color. The pulp is then fed out onto a mesh which drains the water from it. The pulp is then rolled flat and dried.

Materials: Newspapers, window screen attached to a 9" x 12" frame, water, two buckets, a bowl, vegetable dye, a long-handled spoon, rubber gloves, and a rolling pin. (NOTE: the rubber gloves are not necessary for safety, but this is a messy project and the newsprint and vegetable dye may stain your hands temporarily.)

Procedure:

1. Tear the newspaper into small pieces. Place the pieces of newspaper in the bucket and cover them with water. Stir this mixture. Pour off the water as it becomes dark and replace it with clean water. This mixture is your pulp. Let it soak overnight.

2. Pour a cupful of the pulp into the bowl and add two or three drops of food coloring. Mix the food coloring with the pulp.

3. Pour the dyed pulp onto the screen as shown in the diagram at the right. Smooth out the pulp while holding it over the second bucket to drain.

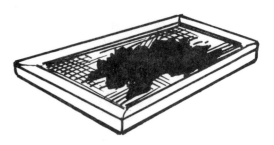

4. Place the frame on top of the bucket or in a sink and flatten the pulp with a rolling pin. Set it aside and let it dry. (This make take a couple of days.)

5. Now you are ready to use your paper to print or to make a picture or a special card.

Printing

The Chinese and Koreans were among the first to use wood blocks to print pictures and words. The process is very similar to linoleum block printing.

Materials: Typing paper, carbon paper, a pencil, a foil pie pan, a linoleum block, a linoleum cutter, ink, and a roller. (NOTE: the linoleum block, cutter, ink, and roller can be purchased at an art supply store.)

Procedure:

1. Trace the outline of the linoleum block onto one sheet of typing paper. Place one sheet of carbon paper ink side up and place the typing paper on top of it with the outline of the linoleum block facing you.

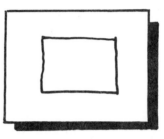

2. Print the message you want to have on your linoleum block inside the outline. Make the print fairly large and keep your message short. You may include a picture, but do not make it too complicated. A simple shape will be easiest to cut.

3. Place the carbon paper with the ink side down on the linoleum block. Turn the typing paper over and you will see your design in reverse on the back of the paper. This is your pattern. Place this pattern directly on top of the carbon paper and the block with the pattern facing you. Trace over your design. When you remove the pattern and the carbon paper, your design should be printed on the linoleum block in reverse.

4. Use your linoleum cutter to cut away any parts of your design that you want to remain white. If you want white letters, cut the letters out. If you want colored letters, cut all around your letters and leave the letters themselves solid.

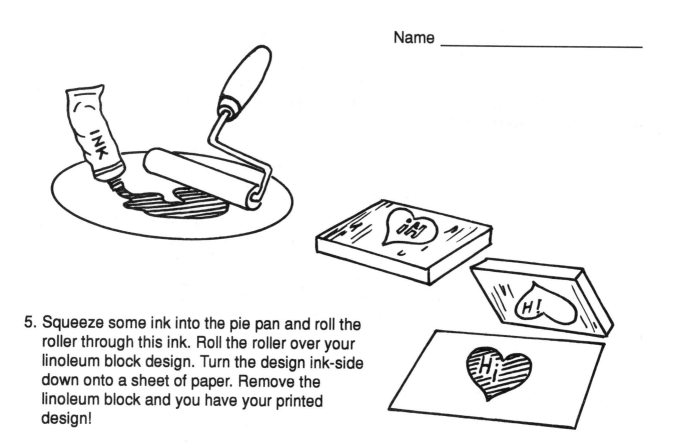

5. Squeeze some ink into the pie pan and roll the roller through this ink. Roll the roller over your linoleum block design. Turn the design ink-side down onto a sheet of paper. Remove the linoleum block and you have your printed design!

The Printing Press

The Chinese and the Koreans invented movable type using porcelain and metal, but their languages have so many alphabet characters that printing was difficult and this printing process did not stay in use. Johannes Gutenberg, who lived over 500 years ago in Mainz, Germany, reinvented movable type and created the first printing press. His press was adapted from an old wine press and, like your linoleum block, it pressed the image onto the paper. Modern printing presses still press the image onto the paper, but these fast-moving machines are a far cry from Gutenberg's original press.

Printing is now one of our chief means of communication. We use it for everything from sales slips to money and bank checks. It is the basis of our educational system. It is one of the top ten industries in the United States.

How does a modern printing press work?

First, the image is typed, drawn, or copied onto a printing plate. The copy plate is moistened and attached to a cylinder called the **plate cylinder.** A water fountain with **dampening rollers** is on one side above the plate cylinder. These rollers keep the plate moist. An ink fountain with **inking rollers** is on the other side of the plate cylinder. These rollers spread the ink on the plate. The plate cylinder rolls against a heavy rubber cylinder called the **blanket cylinder** and leaves the inked mirror image of the plate on this cylinder. The paper is fed through the press against this blanket cylinder and, as it goes through, the inked image is pressed onto the paper.

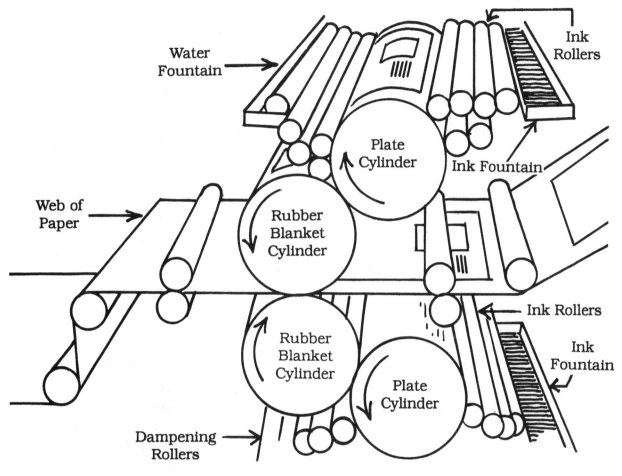

Evaluate:

1. Can you read the image which is on the plate cylinder or is it a mirror image? _____

2. Can you read the image which is on the blanket cylinder or is it a mirror image? _____

Color Printing

Colored pictures are not printed with ink the color of the picture unless the whole picture is just one or two colors. In other words, if you see a sheet of paper with violet printing and violet-colored illustrations, it was probably printed with violet-colored ink. If you see a picture with many different colors in it, it was printed with four basic ink colors—red, yellow, blue, and black. These colors are combined to make all the other colors. The printer makes separate plates for each of these colors by photographing the original using a colored screen that blocks all the colors except the one being used on that plate. The plates are loaded on separate plate cylinders on the printing press. Each plate cylinder has its own blanket cylinder and its own ink fountain. After the paper goes all the way through the press, the four separate colors are combined to make all the colors of the picture. How does this work?

Materials: Watercolors, crayons, or colored pencils.

Color each of the squares below with the colors listed below the square.

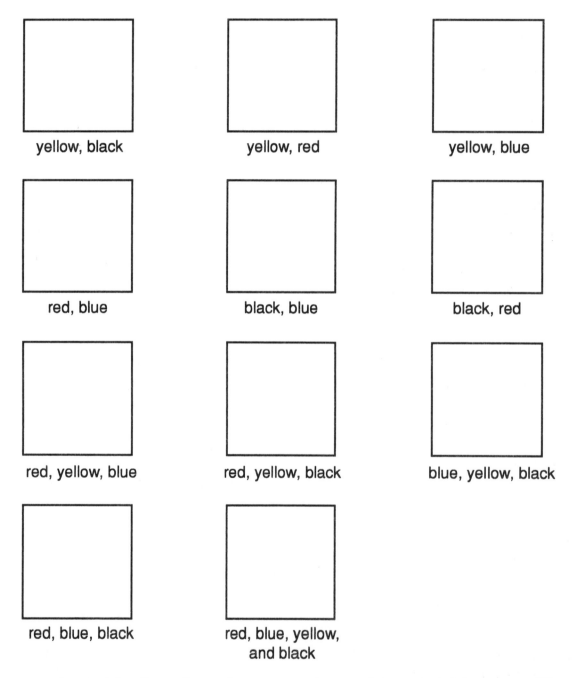

yellow, black

yellow, red

yellow, blue

red, blue

black, blue

black, red

red, yellow, blue

red, yellow, black

blue, yellow, black

red, blue, black

red, blue, yellow,
and black

Can you see how mixing these four colors can produce a picture containing many different colors? _____

The Telephone

Materials: Ten small round magnets or two small bar magnets, posterboard, two lengths of insulated copper wire (one yard each), two Styrofoam cups, several yards of double-stranded wire, typing paper, construction paper, scissors, glue, and electrical tape.

Procedure:

1. Turn a Styrofoam cup upside down on a sheet of typing paper and trace around it twice. Draw a ½" border around this tracing as shown in the diagram at the right.

2. Cut out the two cup covers, cutting around the border line. Notch the covers every half inch, cutting from the border line to the line you traced around the rim of the cup. See the diagram at the right.) These cup covers are the **diaphragms** of the telephone.

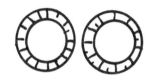

3. If you are using round magnets, place a drop of glue on the tops of eight of the magnets. Glue the magnets together into two stacks of five magnets each. (The stacks should be no more than 1¼" high. Use fewer magnets if they are more than ¼" thick.)

4. Use pattern A on the next page to cut two spool shapes out of posterboard. Tape the patterns at the side to form cylinders and fold the tabs down as shown in the diagram at the right.

5. Remove the insulation from 1" of each end of each copper wire and from each end of the double-stranded wire. Wrap the copper wires around these two spools leaving both ends free. Slide one stack of magnets into the center of each of these spools. This is a **solenoid.**

6. Place a drop of glue on the top of each magnet stack (or on one end of the bar magnets) and glue the cup-cover circles to the magnet stack. Make certain the covers are centered over the stack.

Magnets

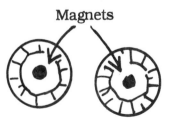

       FS-10169 Science and Technology: How Things Work

7. Cut out pattern B and use it to make two solenoid covers from construction paper. Cut out the sunburst shapes very carefully. Bend the paper on the dotted lines and glue the covers to the bottoms of the solenoid, pulling the ends of the copper wires through the holes.

8. Poke a hole in the bottom of each Styrofoam cup and feed one end of the the two-stranded wire through each hole. Connect one strand of the wire to each of the two wires in each solenoid.

9. Tape the paper covers on the Styrofoam cups with the solenoids inside the cup. Have an assistant take one cup into another room and talk into it. Can you hear anything from your cup?_____

Summary:

The vibrations from your voice vibrate the paper diaphragm on the speaking end of the telephone (modern telephones contain carbon granules and Alexander Graham Bell used an iron disc), setting up a small electrical current in the solenoid. This current is transmitted along the wire and reconverted to vibrations on the diaphragm at the receiving end.

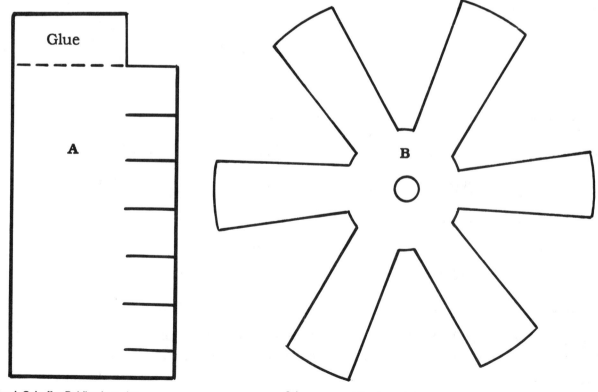

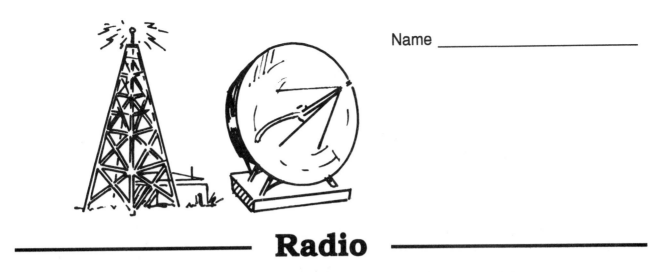

Name _____

Radio

What we call a radio is a radio receiver. The radio station has a transmitter which sends electrical signals to the antenna or the radio tower. These signals cause the antenna to emit radio waves. The radio waves carry the sound to your receiver.

The transmitter broadcasts the radio waves in long-wave, medium-wave, short-wave, or Very High Frequency (VHF) bands. FM radio uses VHF wave bands. AM radio stations use all the other bands. The frequency of radio waves is so high that they are given in **kilohertz** (kHz) or **megahertz** (mHz). Listen for these terms when your favorite radio station gives its call letters and name.

Look at the diagrams below and see if you can label the short-wave, medium-wave, long-wave, and VHF frequencies.

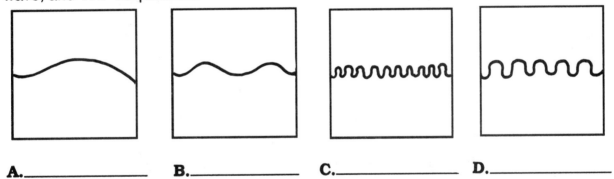

A._____ B._____ C._____ D._____

1. Do all radio stations broadcast the same frequency of radio waves? Why or why not?

_____

_____

2. What is the broadcasting frequency of your favorite radio station? _____

_____

If you are interested in building a radio of your own, consult your library for books such as Hahn, Judith. *How Science Works*. Pleasantville, NY: The Reader's Digest Association, Inc., 1991.

Radar

Radar stands for **RA**dio **D**etecting **A**nd **R**anging. It was developed during World War II as a means of detecting enemy planes and ships. A radio transmitter sends microwave impulses from a rotating antenna. When the waves hit an object, some of them are reflected back to the source. These reflected waves are called an **echo.** Since the speed at which radio waves travel is the same as the speed of light, we can tell how far away the object is by how much time it takes to receive the echo. The same antenna is used for both transmitting and receiving. The signal is beamed out and then the transmitter is turned off to wait for the returning echo. The echo signals are amplified and sent to a tube much like a television tube. This tube sends an electron beam which scans the screen from the center outward in a circle following the rotation of the antenna. If an object sends back an echo of the radar impulses, a "blip" appears on the screen.

You can apply the echo principle of radar to thunderstorms. The time the sound of the thunder takes to travel one mile is roughly the same as the amount of time it takes you to say "one rhinoceros." If a bolt of lightning strikes three miles away, you have time to count "one rhinoceros, two rhinoceros, three rhinoceros."

1. How high would you be able to count if the bolt struck 11 miles away?_____

_____

2. How far away is the thunderstorm if you are able to count up to "nine rhinoceros"?

_____

How does radar work?

Materials: A clear glass baking pan, two large pebbles, a ruler, water, and an 11" x 17" piece of white paper.

Procedure:

1. Fill the pan with water to a depth of ½".

2. Place one pebble near the end of the pan and one pebble a little closer to the middle. Let the water surface smooth out.

3. Gently make a wave at the end of the pan opposite the pebbles. Use the edge of the ruler to push the water.

4. Observe the ripples closely. What happens when they hit the pebbles? _____ _____

5. Which ripples bounce back in the direction of the ruler first, the ripples from the near pebble or the far pebble? _____

Evaluate:

1. The water ripples are like the radar waves. When the waves hit an object, what do they do? _____

2. How can you tell if an object is near or far away? _____

Television

Your television set is a receiver just like your radio. The television station sends video signals on the radio waves. Your television set receives these signals and converts them to pictures.

The picture on a television set is built up from a series of stripes. The movement that you see is really a series of still pictures, and each picture is made up of two scans composed of alternate bands. The camera and picture tubes make 60 scans a second and our brain converts this to moving pictures. How does this work?

The picture is made up of the two scans. The first scan contains only the odd-numbered bands. The second scan contains only the even-numbered bands:

first scan

second scan

Each band is made up of hundreds of tiny elements called **pixels**. The television set has three electron guns, one for the color red, one for green, and one for blue. The television station sends a signal representing the color and brightness of each pixel to the decoder in your television set. The decoder sends this message to one of the three electron guns which flashes the electrons onto the phosphor dots on the screen of your TV, causing it to light up.

If you get very close to a television screen, you may be able to detect these bands. From a distance they merge to make one picture. To see how this works, use colored pencils to complete the picture on the next page. Color the picture according to the numbers of the colors that are listed beside the picture.

red = 1, blue = 2, green = 3

C1	C2	C3	C4	C5	C6	C7	C8	C9	C10	C11	C12	C13	C14	C15	C16	C17	C18	C19	C20	C21	C22
						2									2						
							2							2							
							2							2							
					3	1	3	1	3	1	3	1	3	1	3	1	3				
						1	3	1	1	1	3	1	3	1	1	1	3	1			
					3	1	3	2	3	1	3	1	3	2	3	1	3				
			2		1	1	2	3	2	1	1	1	2	3	2	1	1		2		
		2		2	3	1	3	2	3	1	3	1	3	2	3	1	3	2		2	
					1	1	1	1	1	1	1	1	1	1	1	1	1				
					3	1	3	1	3	3	1	3	3	1	3	1	3				
						1	3	1	3	1	1	1	1	1	3	1	3	1			
					3	1	3	1	3	1	3	1	3	1	3	3	3				
						1	3	1	3	1	3	1	3	1	3	1	3	1			
					3	1			1			1			1	3					
						1	3								3	1					
						3	1	1	1	1	1	3									
								3	3	3	3	3									
							1	3	1	3	1	3	1								
							3	1	3	1	3	1	3								
						3	1	3	1	3	1	3	1	3							
							1	3	1	3	1	3	1	3	1						

Now tape this picture to a wall and walk across the room. Turn around and look at your picture. What color is the face? _____

What color are the eyes? _____

The pictures your television shows are a succession of still shots. The pictures change so rapidly that they appear to be moving. How does this work?

Cut out each of the picture frames on the next page. Color them if you wish, but keep the colors consistent. Arrange them in a stack in the order given and staple them together on the left hand side. Holding the stack by the stapled edge, flip through the pages rapidly. What happens to the image? _____

—Calculators, Computers, and Binary Codes—

A calculator has a place to input the numbers, a place to process the numbers, and a display or place for the answer. It also has a memory bank or place to store the numbers which have been inputted, the directions for processing these numbers, and any calculations required to find the answer. The computer has these same basic units. The difference between the two is the computer program, which can change the computer's memory bank by giving it different sets of instructions. These instructions are given and processed in **binary code.**

Binary code is a two-digit number system. The numerals used are 0 and 1. If you were converting the binary code to decimal numbers, this is how you would do it:

DECIMAL NUMBERS	BINARY NUMBERS	SAY
0	0	zero
1	01	zero-one
2	10	one-zero
3	11	one-one
4	100	one-zero-zero
5	101	one-zero-one
6	110	one-one-zero
7	111	one-one-one
8	1000	one-zero-zero-zero

Now see if you can complete the chart by counting to 12. Remember to think in terms of one-zero and one-one, not ten and eleven.

9 _____

10 _____

11 _____

12 _____

This code can easily be translated into electrical impulses. Zero (0) is no pulse of electricity and one (1) is a pulse of electricity.

The screen of a computer works the same way as the screen of a television. The impulses of electricity from the microprocessor light up each pixel according to the programmed color. See if you can color this picture correctly. Remember, you will first have to translate

         FS-10169 Science and Technology: How Things Work

the binary code numbers back to decimal numbers to know which color is supposed to be in each block.

Color	Decimal Number Code	Binary Number Code
white	1	_____
blue	2	_____
red	3	_____
green	4	_____

10	10	10	10	10	10	10	10	100	10	10	10	10	10	10	10	10	10	10	10	10	10	10	100	100	10	10	
10	10	10	10	10	10	10	100	100	10	10	10	10	10	10	10	10	10	10	10	10	10	10	100	100	10	10	
10	10	10	10	10	10	10	100	100	10	100	100	10	10	10	10	10	10	10	10	10	10	100	100	10	10	10	
10	10	10	10	10	10	100	100	10	10	10	100	100	10	10	10	10	10	10	10	10	10	100	100	10	10	10	
10	10	10	10	10	10	100	100	10	10	10	10	100	10	10	10	10	10	10	10	10	10	100	100	10	10	10	
10	10	10	10	10	100	100	10	10	10	10	100	100	10	10	10	10	10	10	10	10	10	100	100	10	10	10	
10	10	10	10	10	100	100	10	10	10	100	100	10	10	10	10	10	10	10	10	10	10	100	100	10	10	10	
10	10	10	10	10	10	100	100	10	10	100	100	10	10	10	10	01	01	01	10	01	10	10	10	100	100	10	
10	10	10	10	10	10	100	100	10	100	100	10	10	10	10	01	01	01	01	01	01	10	10	10	100	100	10	
10	10	10	10	10	10	10	100	100	100	10	10	10	10	01	01	10	01	01	01	01	10	10	100	100	10	10	
10	10	10	10	10	10	10	100	100	10	10	10	10	10	01	01	01	01	01	01	10	10	100	100	10	10	10	
10	10	10	10	10	10	100	100	10	10	10	10	10	10	10	01	01	01	10	01	10	100	100	10	10	10	10	
10	10	10	10	10	10	100	100	10	10	10	10	10	10	10	10	10	10	10	10	10	100	100	10	10	10	10	
10	10	10	10	10	10	100	100	10	10	10	10	10	10	10	10	10	10	10	10	10	100	100	10	10	10	10	
10	10	10	10	100	100	100	10	10	10	10	10	10	10	10	10	10	10	10	10	100	100	10	10	10	10		
10	10	10	10	100	100	100	10	10	10	10	10	10	10	10	10	10	10	10	100	100	10	10	10	10	10		
10	10	10	10	100	100	100	10	10	10	10	10	10	10	10	10	10	10	10	100	100	10	10	10	10	10		
10	10	10	10	10	100	100	100	10	10	10	10	10	10	10	11	11	11	100	100	10	11	10	10	10	10		
10	10	10	10	10	100	100	100	10	10	10	10	10	10	10	11	11	11	11	11	100	11	10	10	11	10	10	
10	10	10	01	01	01	01	01	10	10	10	10	11	11	11	11	11	11	11	11	11	11	11	10	10	10		
10	10	01	10	01	10	01	10	01	10	11	11	11	11	10	10	01	10	01	100	100	11	11	11	10	10	10	
10	10	10	01	10	01	10	01	10	01	11	11	10	10	10	10	10	10	100	100	10	10	10	10	10	10		
10	10	01	01	01	01	01	01	01	10	10	11	10	10	10	10	10	100	100	10	10	10	10	10	10			
10	10	10	01	01	01	01	01	10	10	10	10	10	10	10	10	10	100	100	10	10	10	10	10	10	10		

Bits and Chips

In 1642, a French mathematician named Blaise Pascal invented a mechanical adding machine which could add and subtract numbers. This machine used toothed wheels to accomplish its calculations. In 1834, an English mathematician named Charles Babbage invented an even larger and more complex calculating machine. This machine, called the Analytical Engine, was the forerunner of the modern computer. It consisted of thousands of gear wheels. It provided a means for giving data and instructions to the machine; it processed the data; it had a device which would print out the answers; and it could be programmed to do more than one thing at a time. Unfortunately, this was before the age of electronics and the design was so complex that Babbage did not live to see his design completed.

1. How are our modern computers different from these early calculating machines? What different uses do we have for our modern computers?

_____

_____

_____

In 1943, the British completed the Colossus. This was the first electronic computer. It was followed by the American ENIAC (Electronic Numerical Integrator and Computer) in 1946. These computers were huge. They were called mainframe computers and were so large that they occupied whole rooms. Smaller transistorized computers were developed in the 1950s and finally, in the 1970s, miniaturization of the electronic equipment allowed the development of smaller and less expensive personal computers or PCs.

2. How has this made computers more useful?

_____

_____

The microchip is the key to the smaller computers. The microchip is an integrated circuit or to put it simply, a large number of connected circuits. It is made up of thousands of electronic components compressed into a tiny piece of silicon. The silicon is less than one centimeter square. The components and the connections between them are not assembled separately and then connected; they are built up in layers.

                   FS-10169 Science and Technology: How Things Work

First, the silicon is made in a cylinder shape. The cylinder is sliced into very thin
(.25 millimeters) discs. The discs are treated to make several hundred microchips. The
wafers are tested and then cut into individual chips. The individual microchips are so small
that they must be inspected under a microscope. The illustration below shows this process.

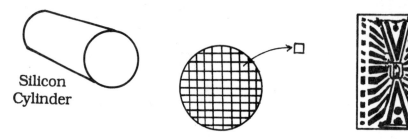

Silicon
Cylinder

Microchip
(magnified)

Do you know these computer terms? Write the letter of the definition in the space before
the matching term.

_____ 1. Software

    a. the space in the computer's memory which is
       filled by one letter or numeral

_____ 2. Cursor

    b. the information which is processed by the
       computer

_____ 3. Mouse

    c. the physical parts of the computer

_____ 4. Byte

    d. the hand control device which directs the cursor

_____ 5. Data

    e. the arrow or highlighted area on the screen

_____ 6. Screen

    f. programs for the computer

_____ 7. Network

    g. a binary digit, a numeral in binary notation
       (0 or 1)

_____ 8. Hardware

    h. the part of the computer that shows the visual
       display

_____ 9. Bit

    i. several computers connected together by a
       modem or telephone

Further Research: What are some of the new medical and technological advances which
use computers? _____

_____

Answer Key

CHAPTER ONE
WEATHER AND NATURAL PHENOMENA

THE WEATHER   **page 5**
1. Accept any reasonable answer, such as we need to know what to wear, we need to be warned of dangerous storms, we need to know when to plant crops...
2. Weather patterns can change swiftly. This year's drought-stricken crops may be next year's flood plain.
3. Weather reporters and national weather forecasters do not always know what weather is coming for a given area. High and low pressure areas can move swiftly or slowly, creating unforeseen changes in the weather.
4. Student response should be based on research. It will vary depending on where you live.
5. In any order, the most important instruments a weather forecaster uses are:
   a. A thermometer which is used to measure the temperature.
   b. An anemometer which is used to measure the speed of the wind.
   c. A barometer which is used to measure the air pressure.
   d. A weathervane, windsock, or other device for determining the direction of the wind.
   e. A hygrometer to determine the amount of humidity in the air.

THERMOMETER   **page 6**
4. As the alcohol warms, it moves up the straw.
5. As the alcohol cools, it moves down the straw.
6. As the alcohol warms, it moves up the straw.
Evaluate:
1. As the alcohol warms, it expands and takes up more space in the straw.
2. The alcohol or mercury expands when it is heated and contracts when it is cooled. When it expands, it takes up more space and appears to move upward. When it contracts, it takes up less space and appears to move downward.

HYGROMETER   **page 7**
5. The response should reflect the student's observations.
6. The dry air tightens the hair, pulling the toothpick with it. The humid air weights the hair down, making it turn the other direction. (Accept any reasonable response.)

BAROMETER   **page 8**
2. The air pushes the plastic wrap down and moves the end of the toothpick with it. The toothpick points up.
3. The suction pulls the plastic wrap up and moves the end of the toothpick with it. The toothpick points down.
Evaluate:
1. Clear, sunny weather is high pressure.
2. Cloudy, damp weather is low pressure; the air pressure decreases.
3. If the needle on a barometer is falling, expect rain.
4. If the needle on a barometer is rising, expect sunny weather.

WINDSOCK   **page 9**
6. The response should reflect the student's observations.
7. When the wind is not blowing hard the windsock hangs down.
8. When the wind is blowing hard the windsock blows out parallel to the ground.
9. When the wind changes direction the windsock changes direction. (TEACHER'S NOTE: This is only true if the hanger moves freely in the ground.)

SEISMOGRAPH   **page 11**
4. The pen makes a squiggly line on the paper when you shake the table.
5. The pen makes a squiggly line with larger hills and valleys when you shake the table harder.
Evaluate:
1. If you feel the tremors of an earthquake, you should go outside to an open place. The inside of a building is the most dangerous place to be.
2. Earthquakes present several dangers; collapsing buildings and falling objects present the most immediate danger, but broken gas lines and water mains may cause fire or flooding immediately afterward.

MEASURING EARTHQUAKES   **page 12**
The shock waves from the 1989 quake were approximately 12 times greater than the 1987 quake.
The difference in terms of destruction was actually closer to 35 times greater.
Evaluate: Some severe earthquakes are less damaging than smaller quakes because they occur in rural, less-populated areas. Metropolitan areas with large numbers of buildings are the hardest hit by earthquakes.

CHAPTER TWO
LIGHT AND LENSES

SUNLIGHT: WHAT IS IT?   **page 17**
1. When you hold the paper in front of the sunlight, the paper still looks white. (Some students may notice a faint yellow tinge.)
2. When you shine the light through the glass, it separates the light into the colors of the spectrum: red, orange, yellow, green, blue, indigo, and violet. (The band at the bottom of the page should show these colors in this order.)
3. When the pencil enters the water, it appears to bend because of refraction.
4. When you place a white cloth over your arm, it reflects the sunlight so your arm does not feel very warm.
5. When you place a black cloth over your arm, it absorbs the sunlight so your arm feels warmer.
6. Black absorbs sunlight.
7. White reflects sunlight.
8. A mirror reflects the sunlight.
9. The response should reflect the student's observations. The image does fade at some point because the mirror absorbs some light and not enough is reflected to be visible.
10. Accept the student response.

INTERFERENCE   **page 19**
1. The pattern should look like this:

3. The pattern should look like this:

6. The colors on the flat shape spread out over the whole shape. The colors on the three-dimensional shapes are blacked out in spots where the light rays cross each other.
7. Accept the student response.

SUNLIGHT AND MIRRORS: THE PERISCOPE   **page 21**
3. The student response should reflect the student's observations.

BENDING LIGHT   **page 23**
2. When the rays of light go through the glass, they converge.
3. When the rays of light go through a convex lens, they converge.
4. When the rays of light go through a concave lens, they spread out.
5. Lenses are used for eyeglasses, cameras, magnifying glasses.
6. When you look through a convex lens the image looks larger.
7. When you look through a concave lens the image looks smaller.

THE MICROSCOPE   **page 24**
4. The response should reflect the student's observations.

A ZOETROPE   **page 26**
6. When the container is spinning rapidly and you look through the viewing hole, the pictures seem to move in a continuous motion like a movie.

LASERS AND BAR CODES   **page 28**
All bar codes are composed of patterns of thick and thin black lines. Each bar code is different.

CHAPTER THREE
HARNESSING ENERGY

WINDMILL RIDER   **page 33**
9. When the person blows on the windmill sails, the bug figure "rides" the unicycle.

WINDMILLS, TURBINES, AND DENTIST DRILLS   **page 35**
1. If he left the sail the same size, the strong winds would blow the wheel too fast and could damage the sail or the weak winds would not be sufficient to turn the mill.
2. The spring type sail works automatically without the manual assistance of the miller.
3. If a windmill is not facing the wind, the sails do not present enough of a surface for the wind to turn them. The sails must be perpendicular to the wind.
5. Accept the student response. Encourage creativity.

WATER POWER   **page 37**
4. When you pour water on the top of the wheel, it turns.

SUN-COOKED S'MORES   **page 39**
4. The heat in the "hot spot" should be sufficient to cook the marshmallow.

SOLAR POWER   **page 40**
Solar power is much more practical for space vehicles because there are no clouds in outer space and nothing to block the sun.

CHEMICAL ENERGY   **page 41**
The temperature inside the jar will rise as the steel wool oxidizes.
Evaluate: As the steel wool oxidizes, the chemical energy is converted to heat energy as shown by the rise in temperature.

COMBUSTION ENGINE   **page 42**
4. When you inflate the balloon, it presses the piston to the top of the cylinder and moves the rods which move the bird.
Evaluate: When the force of combustion presses on the piston, it pushes the piston to the top of the cylinder.

MOTORS   **page 44**
2. The suspended magnet moves until it aligns with its poles opposite that of the wire coil.
3. When you change the flow of the current, it changes the poles of the coil and the magnet turns to make its poles opposite the new poles of the coil.
4. When you switch the current flow back and forth, the magnet turns back and forth trying to match up with the changed poles.
Evaluate:
1. When you change the direction of the current in an electromagnet, you change its magnetic poles.
2. When the current changes direction in one of the electromagnet of a motor, the movable electromagnet moves.

CHAPTER FOUR
ENGINEERING AND PHYSICS

BRIDGE BUILDING   **page 49**
These responses may vary depending on the weight of the book used. The strength of the bridge should increase with each new type of leg/support.
1. Accept the student response. These flat legs should not be able to support much weight. If you add more legs, that will increase the strength, but by very little.
2. Accept the student response. Adding more legs will help some. Placement of the legs will also increase support.
3. Accept the student response.
4. Accept the student response.
Evaluate:
1. The round legs work best.
2. Accept the student response.
3. Some shapes are stronger than others. (Use the information in the TEACHER'S NOTES to explain this.)
4. The shape of a bridge's supports does affect the amount of weight the bridge can carry.

SUSPENSION BRIDGES   **page 51**
5. When you place the weight on the ruler, the shape of the bridge does not change. It can support the weight.
6. When the weight is placed in a different spot, the shape of the bridge does not change.
7. When you tilt the chairs (supports) toward each other, the shape of the bridge changes dramatically.
Evaluate: If the tension is released, the bridge collapses.

BUILDING BUILDINGS   **page 52**
2. You cannot balance a heavy book on these shapes. The legs splay outward when they collapse.
3. The "b" shapes can carry a heavier load.
4. The "c" shapes are equally weak/strong, but the first pair pushes inward when it collapses and the second pair pushes outward. The answers may vary but should reflect the student's observations.
5. The two pairs of shapes do not move the same way. The diagram should look this way:

6. The shapes from "d" can carry a heavier load than the shapes in step 4.
Evaluate:
1. Changing the shape can make a structure stronger.
2. A truss is strong because it is a reinforced triangle shape. The force pressing down is balanced by the forces pulling and pushing the truss together.
3. The closed shapes of "b" and "d" would make the best trusses for the roof of a house.

SHAPE AND STRENGTH   page 54
1. A sheet of paper cannot support much weight at all.
2. When the sheet of paper is folded in an accordion pleat, it can support more weight (at least the weight of a paperback book).
3. A sheet of paper bent in a semicircle can support even more weight.
5. The bridge made of folded paper can support the most weight. Answers will vary but should reflect the student's observations.
Evaluate:
1. Some shapes are stronger than others.
2. The circular shapes and the folded semicircle in step 5 would make the best shapes for supporting bridges and roofs of buildings.
3. The filling of a heavy cardboard carton is shaped like this:

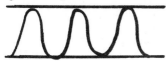

A PUMP   page 56
6. When you push the disc down the tube, it forces air out the outlet door/valve and the door flaps outward.
7. When you pull the straw and the plastic disc up the tube, it pulls air in through the intake door/valve and the door flaps inward.
Evaluate:
1. The outlet valve pumps air into the tire of a bicycle.
2. The intake valve pulls water up from the well.
3. The diagram should look like this:

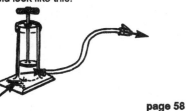

LEVERS   page 58
FIRST-CLASS LEVER:
2. The response should reflect the student's observations.
3. The response should reflect the student's observations.
4. The response should reflect the student's observations.
5. The response should reflect the student's observations.
Evaluate:
1. When the weight on the load end is twice as heavy as the weight on the effort end, the length of the lever on the load end will be twice the length of the lever on the effort end.
2. When the weight on the load end is twice as heavy as the weight on the effort end, the height of the lever on the load end is twice the height of the lever on the effort end.
SECOND-CLASS LEVER:
1. You cannot break the toothpick when it is held at the tip of the fingers.
2. The toothpick breaks easily when it is held close to the palm of the hand.
Evaluate:
1. It is easier to break the toothpick (it requires less force) when the toothpick is near the fulcrum (where the fingers join the palm of the hand).
THIRD-CLASS LEVER:
1. It is not easy to lift the book when the hands are close together.
2. The book is easier to lift when the lifting hand (force) is near the book (load).
Evaluate: A third-class lever is easier to use when the force is nearer to the load.

BRAKES   page 61
1. The correct picture answer is shown at the right. This is the correct choice because the sharp teeth of the bobsled are

needed to create enough friction/resistance on the ice to brake the bobsled. A smooth brake would just slide on the ice.
2. Accept any reasonable answer such as the teeth on the blades of an ice skate, an anchor on a boat, etc.
Procedure:
3. When you close the tweezers, they act as a brake and stop the spinning disc. Disc brakes are much better because they do not slip in wet weather. The heat dries the moisture, keeping the surface dry and making better brake contact.

MOVING HEAVY THINGS   page 63
1. Using one finger, it is hard to move a stack of books.
2. It is easier to move the books once they are rolling on a set of dowels.
3. It is easier to move a stack of books that is on dowel rollers than a stack of books resting flat on the table.
Evaluate:
1. When the books were lying flat on the table, all of the bottom cover of the bottom book was lying flat on the table.
2. When the books were lying on top of the dowel rollers, none of the bottom cover of the bottom book was touching the table and only part of the surface of the dowel was touching the table.
3. When less of the book's surface was touching the table it was easier to move.
4. One way you can reduce friction is by reducing the amount of solid surface areas making contact with each other.

CHAPTER FIVE
LOCOMOTION

BICYCLE GEARS   page 67
6. When you turn the single disc, the wheel turns.
7. When you attach the chain to the larger sprocket, the wheel turns more slowly.
Evaluate:
1. In this chain drive, the smaller sprockets make the wheel move more quickly.
2. The larger sprocket makes the wheel move more slowly.

WATER SKIS   page 69
2. When you drop the needle in the water, it sinks.
3. When you pull the needle slowly, it drags in the water with the point toward the bottom.
4. When you pull the needle in fast circles, it rises, flattens out, and skims the surface of the water.

SAILBOATS   page 70

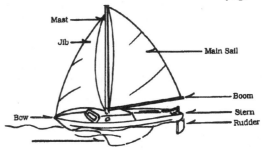

SAILBOAT SAILS   page 71
4. When you blow straight at the boat it moves forward.
5. When you blow straight at the boat it moves forward.
6. When you blow straight at the boat it moves forward. The answers should reflect the student's observations.
Evaluate: The reaching positions actually make the boat move more rapidly and give it more stability.

MOTORBOATS   page 73
8. The boat moves straight ahead when the rudder is parallel to the hull.

9. The boat moves to the right when the rudder is turned to the right.
10. The boat turns to the left when the rudder is turned to the left.

SUBMARINES   **page 75**
1. The water-filled jar sinks.
2. The empty jar floats.
3. The air-filled jar bobs up to the top if you push it under the surface of the water and let it go.
4. The penny sinks.
5. The ball of clay sinks.
6. The clay modeled in the shape of a boat floats.
Evaluate:
1. The empty jar weighs more than the penny.
2. The empty jar covers more surface area than the penny.
3. The water-filled jar is more **dense** than the water.
4. The jar will not sink if it is partly filled with water.
5. The ball of clay is more **dense** than the water.
6. When the clay is spread out into a boat shape, the clay covers a larger area and is less dense in any one spot than the water.

HOT AIR BALLOONS   **page 77**
6. When the balloon is inflated with hot air, it rises.
7. When one penny is placed in the balloon basket, the inflated balloon rises.
8. The answer should reflect the student's observations.
Evaluate:
1. Hot air balloons rise because hot air is **lighter** than cold air.
2. A hot air balloon can carry a limited amount of weight. Yes, there is a limit to the amount of weight it can carry.
3. If the load is too heavy, the balloon will not rise.
4. If you were in a balloon and it was not rising high enough, you could throw out extra weight to make it rise higher.

GLIDERS   **page 80**
2. When you blow hard against the upper surface of a sheet of paper, the paper rises.
3. Plane B should fly longer and farther.
4. Accept the student response.
Evaluate: The shape of the plane affects the length and speed of its flight.

AIRPLANES   **page 82**
2. Accept the student response. The plane should fly in a straight line.
3. Folding the ailerons up or down makes the plane turn and curve.

HELICOPTERS   **page 83**
3. When you pull the string rapidly, the spool and propeller rise in the air.
Evaluate: A rapidly rotating propeller or rotor blade pulls the helicopter off the ground.

BOOMERANGS   **page 84**
Procedure: The boomerangs fly out away from the thrower and then turn and curve back toward the thrower.
Evaluate: The helicopter would be turned backward and toward the ground if the blades were stationary and would possibly crash.

CHAPTER SIX
COMMUNICATION

PRINTING   **page 89**
Evaluate:
1. You can read the image on the plate cylinder. It is not a mirror image.
2. You cannot read the image on the blanket cylinder. It is a mirror image.
Accept the student response.

THE TELEPHONE   **page 93**

9. The student should be able to hear the person speaking on the other end although it may be very faint.

RADIO   **page 95**
The waves should be labeled as follows:
A. long-wave, B. medium-wave, C. VHF, D. short-wave

1. All radio stations do not broadcast on the same frequency of radio waves. If they did, you would hear a jumble of overlapping programs on your receiver. Occasionally, you are able to receive transmissions from two stations with very similar frequencies. When this happens, you have a jumble of the two programs playing simultaneously on your receiver.
2. Accept the student response.

RADAR   **page 96**
1. If the bolt struck 11 miles away, you should be able to count to "11 rhinoceros."
2. If you can count to "9 rhinoceros," the thunderstorm is approximately 9 miles away.
4. When the ripples hit the pebbles, some bounce back.
5. The ripples from the near pebble bounce back first.
Evaluate:
1. When the radar waves hit an object, some of the waves bounce back to the source.
2. The echo waves bounce back from near objects more rapidly than from far objects.

TELEVISION   **page 98**
The face should appear brown from a distance and the eyes should appear blue-green. When you flip through the stack of pictures, the image appears to move.

CALCULATORS, COMPUTERS, AND BINARY CODES
                                                  page 101
9 is 1001 or one-zero-zero-one
10 is 1010 or one-zero-one-zero
11 is 1011 or one-zero-one-one
12 is 1100 or one-one-zero-zero
The colors are as follows:

COLOR	BINARY NUMBER	
white	01	(zero-one)
blue	10	(one-zero)
red	11	(one-one)
green	100	(one-zero-zero)

The picture should be colored as follows: a white fish, a red crab, and green seaweed in a blue sea.

BITS AND CHIPS   **PAGE 103**
1. We use computers as word processors, for launching and flying space shuttles, for games, for internal medicine, for unning trains, for internal engine auditing . . .
2. Small computers can be purchased and used by individuals not just large corporations.

1. f	4. a	7. i
2. e	5. b	8. c
3. d	6. h	9. g